Success Uncovered

Research: James Miller, Helen Sykes, Melanie Jarvis-Vaughan, Peter Guthridge, Mark Gregory and Shawn Willis

Edited By Kizzi Nkwocha (c)

Originally published with love, respect and admiration by Athena and Mithra Publishing 2015

This revised edition is published in 2017.

Sponsored by My Entrepreneur Magazine

All rights reserved. No part of this work may be reproduced or transmitted in any form or by any means, electronic or mechanical, including photocopying, recording, or by any information storage or retrieval system, without the prior written permission of the copyright owner and the publisher.

This book is presented solely for educational and entertainment purposes. The author and publisher are not offering it as legal, accounting, or other professional services advice. While best efforts have been used in preparing this book, the author and publisher make no representations or warranties of any kind and assume no liabilities of any kind with respect to the accuracy or completeness of the contents and specifically disclaim any implied warranties of merchantability or fitness of use for a particular purpose.

Neither the author nor the publisher shall be held liable or responsible to any person or entity with respect to any loss or incidental or consequential damages caused, or alleged to have been caused, directly or indirectly, by the information or programs contained herein. No warranty may be created or extended by sales representatives or written sales materials. Every company is different and the advice and strategies contained herein may not be suitable for your situation. You should always seek the services of a competent professional.

Also by Athena Publishing

Escape Your 9-5 And Do Something Amazing
Customer Service
SocMed: Social Media For Business
How To Start A Business With Little Or No Cash
Facebook For Business
Social Media Marketing: Write Up your Tweet
Getting Your Business LinkedIn
It's That Easy! Online Marketing 3.0
Business, Business, Business!
Mind Your Own Business
Insiders Know-how: Running A PR Agency
Insiders Know-how: Caring For Your Horse
Energy Efficiency
Social PR

Visit www.athenapublishing.com

"Success is walking from failure to failure with no loss of enthusiasm."
Kizzi Nkwocha

"Stop chasing the money and start chasing the passion."
Tony Hsieh

"Take up one idea. Make that one idea your life--think of it, dream of it, live on that idea. Let the brain, muscles, nerves, every part of your body, be full of that idea, and just leave every other idea alone. This is the way to success."
Swami Vivekananda

"All our dreams can come true if we have the courage to pursue them."
Walt Disney

The Inspiring thought leaders who contributed to this book:

Dr. John Demartini, Jeanine Joy, Janelle Ryan, Meiyoko Taylor,
Dr. Emer MacSweeney, Rev. Marilyn Redmond, Jane Turner, Deborah Lange, Louise Plant, Naomi Holtring, Divya Bannerjee, Arpan Roy, Neville Stone, Louisa Forrest, Matt Bolton-Alarcon, Petros Galanoulis, Sarah Cordiner and Alexandra Tonks.

Success Uncovered is sponsored by My Entrepreneur Magazine. Visit: www.myentrepreneurmagazine.com

Gems Inside

About Kizzi Nkwocha	14
The Turning Point Of My Teaching Success Happened When I Least Expected It	16
How To Turn Your Dream Into A Reality	28
Success Is An Inside Job	40
Develop A Successful And Resilient Mindset	48
Beyond The Barriers To Success	66
Managing Stress Is My Key To Success	81
Success By Choice	93
How Do You Measure Your Success?	114
Wellbeing Through Harmony	122
The Three Pillars Of Success	134
Unlock Your Personal Power	144
10 Steps To Reinvention In The 21st Century	155
How To Maximise Your Inner Creative Genius	168
A Non-Negotiable Decision	182
(Re) Defining Success	192
It Takes A Long Time To Become An Overnight Success	206
Vitality And Vibration - How To Manage Your Energy To Create The Life You Want!	212
Re:Cognition Health And Success	232

About Kizzi Nkwocha

Kizzi Nkwocha made his mark in the UK as publicist, journalist and social media pioneer.

As a widely respected and successful media consultant Nkwocha has represented a diverse range of clients including the King of Uganda, mistresses of President Clinton, Amnesty International, Pakistani cricket captain Wasim Akram, campaign group Jubilee 2000, Dragons Den businessman, Levi Roots and world record teenage sailor, Michael Perham.

Nkwocha has also become a well-known personality on both radio and television. He has been the focus of a Channel 4 documentary on publicity and has hosted his own talk show, London Line, on Sky TV.

He also co-presented a weekly current affairs program in Spain on Radio Onda Cero International and both radio and TV shows in Cyprus.

His books have included the fiction novel, Heavens Fire, the business guide books: Business, Business, Business!, Mind Your Own Business, Insiders Know-How: Public Relations and the international bestseller SocMed: Social Media For Business.

Nkwocha publishes the online publications:
The Property Investor (www.tpimag.com)
My Entrepreneur Magazine (www.myentrepreneurmagazine.com)
The Sussex Newspaper (www.thesussexnewspaper.com)
My Logistics Magazine (www.mylogisticsmagazine.com)
My Well-being Magazine (www.mywellbeingmagazine.com).

Follow Kizzi on Twitter: https://twitter.com/kizzinkwocha

The Turning Point Of My Teaching Success Happened When I Least Expected It

The turning point of my present teaching success occurred unexpectedly when I was a teenager. In fact, at that moment of my life, it seems I was doing everything in my power to avoid all chances of having a life considered successful in the field of education. As a stereotypical unemployed, high school dropout and stoned hippie surfer living in a tent in Haleiwa, Hawaii, my idea of learning at the time was solely consisting of staring at pictures of fabulous waves and hot babes and helping a famous surf board maker shape his North Shore surfboards.

Then one night, when I was 17 years old and near one of the lowest periods of my life, I attended a presentation by a very special and inspired man. Although there were other attendees, I felt he was speaking specifically to me, and in a way I had never been spoken to before. He told us – me – that deep down inside all of us – me – there was a genius, a seed of greatness, an inner power, and a potential to achieve extraordinary things.

This man who uttered the seemingly improbable to me was Paul C. Bragg, the remarkable individual who has inspired so many. Had we not met that night, I most likely would not be where I am today. No, let me revise that: I most definitely would not be where I am today. The exact moment that my life turned around and put me on the path to my personal growth and life success was the moment where he and I met and I was ready to listen. This was the first night in my whole life that I dared to think I might actually become intelligent and able to overcome the learning issues and other obstacles I had been born with and myself placed in my life.

A singular moment, an exact location, a particular person, all three intertwined into a moment that could not have been duplicated, resulting in an epiphany that could have come no other way. The course of my life changed, without doubt, with an encounter with one exact man at one exact time in one exact location.

The inspiring thing is, this moment of my turnaround, of my journey to success, wasn't actually the beginning. It was the culmination of synchronous events and situations that had already happened in a universal attempt to bring me a greater degree of awareness or enlightenment, and it was also but one of thousands of moments and encounters yet to come to keep me on my path.

You see, if I hadn't gone to see Paul C. Bragg at a local event that evening, I never would have had that encounter. And if I hadn't seen an inviting flyer on the glass door of the Vim and Vigor health food store, I never would have known about Paul and his appearance in the first place. And if a Good Samaritan of a lady hadn't found me nearly dead in my tent and help me recover and take me to that health food store, I never would have seen the flyer. And if I hadn't been violently ill while lying in a tent in the jungle near the beach, this helpful woman wouldn't have heard me moaning or been compelled or inspired to help me recover or take me to that health food store to heal me. And if that woman hadn't been in a place in her own life to desire to help a young, ill man in distress, she may never have stopped to assist. And if I would not have eaten the toxic seeds prior, I wouldn't have been sick in the first place. And…

And so it goes.

A thousand variables. A million possibilities. Billions of potential outcomes. All coalesced into that synchronous moment at a point when I most definitely wasn't expecting.

Lesson number one of initiating success when you're not expecting it, is, take the synchronous moment. Each moment of possibility that presents itself to you, grab it or allow it to grab you. You will probably never know how many forces for how long have been working to bring you that moment.

An additional inspiring thing about my life-changing moment: meeting this man who inspired me – while everything that it was – was not everything. Yes, I was inspired; after our encounter, I wanted to turn my life around and I wanted to succeed as a world-traveling teacher. But he didn't tell me which path to choose; all he had to do was let me know that there was a path, and that I was worthy to walk upon it. If it had stopped there, if I had just allowed that one moment to be the only moment, success may have still come to me. I might have buckled down and continued my craft and eventually become the best surfboard maker in the world. A path to be certain, but not the one meant for me.

That evening, my eyes were open to the possibilities of walking a path. But later, I closed my eyes, and I saw where that path would lead me. I envisioned I was speaking in front of a large, captivated audience overlooking a giant square. And it was that exact moment where I set out on my inspiring teaching journey.

Lesson two: as cliché as it sounds, follow your inspired vision. I did, literally. There was nothing in my past that gave the slightest indication I could orate in front of a vast crowd, or that I would even want to. But my vision that night showed me a future that has quite literally come true. Paul C. Bragg has inspired many to become great in their fields; his followers have included Jack LaLanne, Donald Trump, and Steve Jobs. Those who have listened to him have become captains of industry, and gifted speakers in their own right, and leaders of corporations and government, and entrepreneurs, and visionaries. But he didn't point to each one and say, "You will invent this," or "You will preside over that," or "John, you will become an inspirational speaker." That night, my epiphany or vision showed me what was buried in my mind and heart, and I followed it.

I was especially fortunate in that my path became clear to me that night; I'd had a vision of a single goal of teaching, and I found myself committed to achieving that goal. Many others are not so fortunate. Even after receiving an epiphany like I did, that they were worthy of greater things in life than they had allowed, they may not know how to take that next step – the first on their new path – because they may not have had a clear vision of the end result. Don't misunderstand me; a vision is not always seen or required, and no end result always needs to be particularly visualized, to achieve some forms of success. Sometimes a path may need to be taken with a state of unclarity or on blind faith alone. Those who walk upon hot coals don't necessarily burn their feet, but they won't know until they have tried.

Before my inspired vision, I hadn't set out to become a researcher, writer, or teacher. But every journey does indeed begin with a single step, and mine was the desire to finally learn to overcome my self-imposed illiteracy and learn to read. Upon turning 18, I returned to Texas, sat through and guessed at the answers of a General Equivalency Diploma exam and somehow passed. I did the same for the A.C.T. exam and likewise miraculously passed. I then attempted a summer school college class on American history and failed miserably. I received a 27 and I needed at least a 72 to pass.

It's strange how one little chink in the track can derail your entire life vision or plan, isn't it? As humans, we tend to want things now, in the moment, in the ecstasy of immediate gratification, and when we don't get it, we're willing to throw away every accomplishment we've done leading up to it in an instant. This is the mindset that got me in trouble in my youth in the first place, and my first true failure after starting my path to being intelligent and an inspired teacher threatened to have history repeat itself.

With that so-called failure, I momentarily lost sight of my vision and doubted whether I could truly fulfill my vision; that is, until my mother came home and found me crying on the sunken living room floor. I told her that I had bombed the history test and that my first grade teacher was probably right after all, and that I would never be able to read, or write, or communicate, or go very far or amount to very much in life.

My mother stood silently for a moment and then stated; "Son, whether you become a great teacher and travel the world as you envision, or whether you return to Hawaii and ride giant waves and make surfboards, or whether you return to the streets and panhandle as a bum, I just want you to know that your dad and I are going to love you no matter what you do."

Upon hearing this my hand went into a fist and I looked up and saw my inspired vision and said to myself; "I am going to master these things called reading, studying, and teaching, and I am going to do whatever it takes, travel whatever distance, and pay whatever price to give my service of teaching and love across the world." I then hugged my mom and entered my room and grabbed her dictionary and committed to memorizing and learning the definitions of thirty words a day, every day.

With her special, heartfelt words, my mother let me know that, in her eyes, I was already a success, that she knew I could succeed in anything I attempted. I had come home defeated and crying, and my mother let me know that whether I decided to become a great teacher and travel, or if I chose to ride the waves on the North Shore, that she and my dad would love me no matter what. Had I desired to become that surfboard maker, her words told me that I'd be the most successful surfboard maker in the world, and that would be fine with her.

Her words galvanized me and reaffirmed my commitment to succeeding in my life plans. Had I listened to my own – and my first grade teacher's – words in my head, I might never have continued on my path and instead sought an "easier" success that didn't require higher education. That exact moment of so-called failure became a turning point for my teaching success because my mother showed me unconditional love. I made the commitment that night to not let anything on the face of the earth stop me from achieving my dream. I would travel whatever distance, pay whatever price, to spread to others the message of the unconditional love that my mother had shown me. Today, I literally travel 365 days a year in that quest to spread the message, that's how profound the impact of those special words had on me.

Two things that helped me learn to read and retain vocabulary were her daily testing and my keeping a checklist of what worked – and what didn't work – each day. Her caring, coupled with my reflection, allowed me to keep track of each success and failure, which I discovered is essential to grow as I took my journey.

Another thing that helped – indeed, a vital component – was the support and challenge of my own mother. She would be sure to test me on my thirty words a day. For my birthday, she asked me what I wanted as a present. I told her, "I want the greatest writings and teachings from the greatest minds on the earth." I'll never forget her response – "Are you sure you don't just want a t-shirt?" – but her belief in me, inspired by my own fervent commitment to becoming literate, prompted her to contact her brother, who was a former professor at the Massachusetts Institute of Technology. He in turn sent me a literal truckload of books; two huge crates – six feet on each side – containing thousands of works of literature.

The third lesson of allowing success into your life when you least expect it and have other ideas is, sometimes let others take matters into their own hands for you. My literacy would have come eventually, certainly, on my own, with my mother's single battered dictionary. But the actions of my mother and uncle jumpstarted that literacy a thousand-fold. Reading all these books – and rest assured I read every one – is what prompted me to integrate the thoughts, ideas, and philosophies of several luminaries into my own personal guide to self-mastery and success that would eventually become the Demartini Method, my series of books, lectures, and workshops designed to bring the greatest possible results to countless thousands of those who follow it. All this because I didn't ask for a t-shirt for my birthday.

Thomas Edison once said, "I have not failed; I've just found 10,000 ways that won't work." Humorous, but true on many levels. So-called failure or its feedback is essential to success. I don't say this to be blithe. On the contrary, the immobilizing fear of failure is a guaranteed way to ensure failure, and I maintain that one must face so-called failure – not just once but scores of times – if one must ever hope to achieve true and lasting success.

Emboldened by my newfound literacy, I began to pass my tests and rise in my classes. As my college life progressed, I found myself reading 18 or 20 hours a day. With my nose buried in books, it took a while to look up to eventually discover that others were following me around, curious about what I was reading and why I was so captivated. I suddenly found myself transitioning from a solitary scholar to a popular educator. I began unofficially teaching post-class classes to nearly 150 fellow students, passing forward what I had read on to them.

This is another example of success finding me when I wasn't expecting it; instead of being a solitary bookworm, I soon found myself surrounded by others hungry for the knowledge I myself was learning. The lesson here is simple: look around sometimes. The old saying goes that success sometimes knocks on our door and we have to open it to see it. I believe that frequently success isn't that obvious, and sometimes it merely walks alongside you on the campus quad. You don't have to answer a knock to see it; sometimes you just need to look up.

Success is an ongoing journey with no real end. By all traditional definitions of the word, I am considered successful. Do I wish for even greater success? I resoundingly say yes, because the greater my own success, the more I am allowed to spread the word to more people in more locations that would otherwise be closed to the loving and inspired service I can provide.

Sir Isaac Newton once said, "If I have seen farther, it is because I have stood on the shoulders of giants." I utterly feel where old Isaac was coming from. Paul C. Bragg was one of many visionaries and mentors I have encountered in my journey. I recall once meeting Howard Hughes himself. I was 14 years old while hitchhiking through El Paso, Texas. At the time, I didn't take his words to heart when he told me, "Young man, you learn how to read. For there are only two things that no one can take away from you and those are your love and wisdom." One might think that this would have been my turning point; the right man and the right words. However, not all the prerequisites for my undivided attention were in place, and those words were tucked away for three more years until I was ready to embrace their intent. Later in my journey, I met another great man who was 37 years old who had achieved six doctorate degrees in his own path of becoming a student of life. These great men – and many others I have encountered – have been secondary catalysts to my success. Even when you're not ready or expecting the next catalyst for success – as was my case in El Paso – I somehow retained the words and deeds of others who have been successful; for later I was ready to receive and implement them. Back then, Hughes' words hadn't completely touched me; however, today, many decades later, it cannot be denied that my central message revolves around the love of wisdom and the wisdom of love.

You tend to hear what you're listening for and find what you're looking for. There's the old adage/joke, "Why do I find my keys at the last place I look for them?" The answer is simple: because when you find what you're looking for, you generally stop looking. Perhaps if you continued your search after you found your keys, you could have found so much more that you hadn't even realized you were looking for. The same goes with success. After I completed my formal primary, secondary and tertiary education and formed my own company and educational institute, I could have labeled that as my success and stop looking there and then. But by continuing my search and research, without even knowing exactly all of what I was looking for, I found much more than a set of car keys; I found levels of success that I could not have ever conceived of or envisioned initially that were there waiting to be found.

What, in particular did I find? For one thing, I found that your personal journey begins with a single action step, and what that perfect starting point is revolves around what you truly value – what is most meaningful, inspiring and important to your life at that moment. I discovered that every human lives by specific set of priorities or values. These values can fall under one or more of the following seven areas of life – spiritual, mental, vocational, financial, familial, social and physical. All seven areas and their quests for empowerment and development are universal and essential in order for people to realize their fullest potentials and successes. They can be their greatest asset or albatross, depending on how they are prioritized and acted upon.

Your highest priority value, which could be concentrated in one or more of the seven areas of your life, can arise from and is determined by what you perceive as most missing or void in your life. The importance you place on each of your values determines how you perceive and how you act in your life, and therefore they determine your immediate path. Since your hierarchy of values change over time, your path can therefore evolve over time. Your present purpose or mission for life will reflect your present highest value. Those who set goals that align with their own highest values find themselves in a self-perpetuating circle of progress and success. Those who set goals that are less soul-feeding find themselves in more of a whirlpool or quicksand from which there is no easy extraction.

I found that I deeply loved helping people find their highest priorities or most intrinsic values so they could more efficiently achieve their most inspiring outcomes. I learned that when their goals were properly aligned with their highest values, the executive center of their brain kicked in and there were actual physical responses like receiving clarity of vision; the brain becomes more capable of envisioning a desired outcome, executing the prioritized action steps to achieve that outcome. Prioritizing is essential to success; if you don't fill your day with high priority actions that inspire you, your day will be filled with low priority distractions that don't.

I found that people need to give themselves permission to live their lives according to their highest values, and that I was in a unique position to help them identify these most meaningful priorities, to help them structure their lives to live by them and to help them give themselves the right or permission to do so.

I found what I call the "ABCDs of Negativity" – Aggression/Anger, Blame/Betrayal, Criticism/Challenge, Despair/Depression – are feedback mechanisms to your consciousness to let yourself know whenever you are not congruent and when what you are doing is not working. These ABCDs can be dissolved once you set goals that are congruent with your true highest values.

I discovered a vital component of self-awareness, self-fulfillment, and success: There is no way a person can highly value themselves as long as they're attempting to live according to someone else's values. If you compare yourself to others, imitate others, subordinate to others, and live in the shadows of others and attempt to live according to their life, you are setting yourself up for defeat. As the great poet Ralph Waldo Emerson said, envy is ignorance, imitation is suicide, and a man must take himself for better or for worse and appreciate who he truly is.

These are all things I found after I had already achieved what could be termed traditional success. That is a vital lesson that cannot be understated: never stop looking. Continue to expand your search for the next thing, even if you initially have little idea what it is. With enough self-awareness, you'll know it when you find it. As long as you are green, you are growing – as soon as you ripen, you rot.

Don't mistake me: success is rarely accidental. To specify, yes, there have been many wonderful examples of accidental successes – the discovery of penicillin and sticky-note adhesive, for instance – but to sustain that success takes effort.

As for your own success, it won't come by someone else waking up in the morning with a desire to fulfill your highest values and bring you contentment and success at the cost of their own. It comes by your own openness, your own questing and questioning, your own fortitude and resolve. Your success is entirely dependent on you, even if you're temporarily looking in all the wrong places for it. The secret is to leave yourself open to all possibilities. In those possibilities, there are myriads of chances of so-called failure, but the opportunities for success are mixed right in among them.

From my experience, I have found that the perfect first step on the path to success is to undergo a highest value determination process. Take a true, hard look at all aspects of your life – the physical ones and the intangible – and look at what your life demonstrates as truly most important and prioritize what your life shows you value. Make a commitment to prioritize how you live daily that will result in your fulfillment of your highest values, what I term "The Values Factor." Every day, list the seven highest priority action steps you need to accomplish each day to bring you another step closer to achieving your dream.

Once that first step is taken, self-certitude is more likely and crucial. Affirm to yourself daily, "It's impossible for me to not fulfill my inspired mission; for it is my destiny." Be certain even in those moments seeming to be filled with uncertainty: question what you don't know, and know that the quality of your life is determined by the quality of your questions you ask yourself. Next, allow yourself to fully embrace that you are worthy of your desired success, that it is ready to find you and that you are ready to be found. Your mindset is of utmost importance and must never cease; the world around you reflects the world within you, and vice versa. Tell yourself, "I now give myself permission to do something extraordinary on planet earth" and know that, in return, everything is on the way, not in the way. Whatever you think and thank about, you bring about.

Finally, open your mind, your heart, your eyes, your ears, for ever-greater possibilities. Be open to anything and everything that helps you on your journey to success, for you never know what exact moment mingles with the proper person at the correct location to bring you your own turning point.

Master plan for your success, but also plan for your success to have other viable alternative ideas on how it will be realized by you. That turning point may come with something as obvious as a rare synchronous encounter with an inspirational mentor because you saw his flyer on a glass door because you had fallen ill and someone cared enough to assist you. Or it may be more subtle, like the day you picked up a book and reached a chapter entitled The Turning Point of My Teaching Success Happened When I Least Expected it...

Dr. John Demartini

About the author

Dr. John Demartini – who literally spends 365 days a year traveling all around the planet – is a noted educator, business consultant, author and founder of The Demartini Institute, a private research, education and service institute he founded in 1982 in Houston, Texas. A globally renowned inspirational speaker, Demartini, who was featured in the acclaimed book and movie The Secret, is the author of 40 books published in over 29 different languages. He has produced over 60 CDs and DVDs covering subjects such as development in relationships, wealth, education and business.

How To Turn Your Dream Into A Reality

Sarah rolls over, reaches out from under the warm bedding and pushes snooze on her alarm clock. Monday again. Does she really have to haul her butt into that soul sucking office for another week? She rolls over for another 6 minutes of denial. She dreams of opening her own bakery, but she doesn't know how.

Rod puts down his lunch and looks longingly at the corner office. He can see his former colleague, now CEO, with his feet on the desk talking into his phone. He's smiling so it must be good news – no doubt another profitable deal has been confirmed. How did he do it? How did he propel from salesman to number one executive in such a seemingly short amount of time. When will it be Rod's turn for a promotion?

Laura applauds the runners as they make their way across the finish line. Running a marathon is something to be celebrated. On January 1st for the past five years, Laura has vowed this will be the year she runs a marathon. But somehow it never happens. Why is that?

Do any of these scenarios sound familiar? Is there something you've been aching to bring into your life? It may be a new dream or something you've fantasized about for many years. But it just doesn't show up. Other people seem to have all the luck.

No, they don't. Everyone on the planet has exactly the same amount of 'luck' as you. What they have done is turned their dream into a goal, then created a strategy to make it appear. Sound simple? Well it kind of is. Once you know how.

I have a dream to go to Bora Bora. I want to stay in one of those huts that are built over the water – the ones that have a glass floor so I can gaze at the colourful fish gliding through the crystal clear water. I have another dream to cruise through Alaska. Both these things are on my so called bucket list.

Both these things are dreams of mine. And for now, I'm happy for them to stay that way.

You see, there are no plans in place to visit either of these destinations. No dates set. No flights, accommodation nor cruise has been booked. I don't even have a brochure in my possession – for either of them.

Because I currently have personal and professional GOALS and they are what I'm working on right now.

You can have all the dreams in the world – but if you haven't turned them into a goal, sub goals and an action plan – that's where they will stay. In your dreams.

So how do you do that?

Step 1: Become a visionary in your own life.

By this I mean you get crystal clear on what it is you wish to bring into your reality. One way to do this is by using all your modalities – seeing, hearing, smelling, tasting, touching, *and experiencing* what you wish to create.

Visual Mental Rehearsal, or VMR, is one of the most effective ways to experience your desire.

Find a quiet room where you will not be disturbed for at least 30 minutes. Sit or lie in a relaxed position and close your eyes. Start to take longer, deeper breaths, relaxing your body with each outward breath. Drop out of your busy mind, away from the 'do list' that may be occupying your thoughts and take yourself into a day of your 'perfect' life. There are a couple of ways you can do this – walk yourself through your perfect day from morning until evening or stepping through a door into your perfect life and observing what's inside!

Or any other way that feels best for you.

Whichever way you decide to experience your perfect life, ensure you use ALL your modalities. As you move through the exercise, note the following (feel free to add your own):

- What can you see in your perfect life?
- What can you hear?
- Who is in your perfect life? How are they treating you? How do you feel around them?
- What can you smell?
- How does your body feel?
- Can you taste anything?
- What are you doing in your perfect life?
- What kind of person are YOU in your perfect life?
- How is your mood?
- How do you FEEL in your perfect life?

Stay in your perfect life for as long as you like. Stay there until all your senses have been heightened and the experience is SO POWERFUL it feels like your reality. You can move through this activity more than once.

When you are satisfied that your vision is CRYSTAL CLEAR make detailed notes. Remember you are writing the next chapter of your life! Be precise.

Step 2: Create a Powerful Reminder of your Vision

The two ways I love to remind me of my vision are daily journaling and vision boards. Today I want to outline how to create a vision board that is motivational AND magic.

Why do I love vision boards?

Because thoughts are pictures in our mind.

When we focus on pictures they create feelings and emotions; for example I cannot watch the evening news as the pictures that flash onto my screen can be distressing, but gazing at photos of those I love brings happiness and joy into my heart.

It's feelings and emotions that motivate us to take action. We tend to move towards things that make us feel excited and full of energy and away from things that suck the energy from our soul.

I love my vision board. It sits on my desk where I can look at it every minute I'm working at my computer, if I wish to. I've attached mantras I believe in, photos of times in my life I've felt really happy and blessed, pictures that represent achievements I've been proud of, random words I'd like to live by and pictures of things I wish to bring into my life. How does the vision board work for me?

It anchors my vision and gives it clarity.

- Have you ever heard the saying that people don't get what they want because they don't know what they want? Sometimes that is true.
- Helps quieten the internal chatter of my mind and move through the external forces of life – those things that pull us in every direction when we get out of bed in the morning.
- No matter what's going on during my day, when I look at my vision board it brings me back to what my focus is.

It motivates me to take action.

- I have deliberately included a huge photo of a fit and healthy woman from a running magazine. She gets me out of my seat and moving my body.
- I have pictures that represent the direction I want my business to go and those reminders propel me to take action.

It makes me feel good.

I think one of the secrets to a good vision board is including things that make you feel proud and happy, not just material things that you want in your life. I have photos of my family and friends who inspire and support me.

As we talked about before, we all have thoughts and thoughts are pictures. When we focus on pictures it creates feelings within us and those feelings motivate us to take action towards something. Do we just focus on the vision board and wait for the universe to manifest all our dreams and desires into our life? Some people believe so, but I prefer to use my vision board to move me to an active state of achieving my next goal.

Tips for creating your own vision board

- There are no rules – this is YOUR vision board so create it as you wish. You can use corkboard, a magnetic whiteboard, cardboard, paper or electronic programs
- You can use any materials you wish – photos, magazine words and pictures, invitations, drawings, stickers.......and anything else you can think of.
- Focus on how you want to feel – rather than just what you want.
- Work out your goals first, and then put anything on your board that moves or inspires you to take action towards achieving them.
- This is YOUR vision board so you decide if you want one large one or numerous mini ones scattered around your house.
- Allocate the time in your day to really create something that is meaningful to you.
- Enjoy the process - it really is heaps of fun!

If you take the time and enjoy creating a vision board that is motivational, you often find it's a little bit magic as well!

Step 3: Turn Your Vision to a Goal

Why is turning your vision into a goal such an important part of bringing your dream to reality? Because goals are a place to come from – not get to. When a goal is in place we have something almost tangible in front of us.

We set goals for ourselves all day, every day. A goal to get to work on time. A goal to feed yourself and your family as healthily as you can. A goal to meet your friends for dinner at 7.30pm at the new restaurant on High Street tonight.

I just want to pause here for a second. Let's face it – you have a default future. You have a future that will roll out without much effort from you. Many millions of people live quite happily this way. But I'm going to go out on a limb and say that's not you – the reason you are reading this book, and more specifically this chapter, is because you have a dream you want to bring into your reality.

So let's get you back to goal setting.

World class athletes, successful business people and high performers across all fields set goals.

Why?

- You can't achieve a goal without first going through a goal setting process.
- Goals create a road map for your success.
- Written goals help you focus on where you're going and what changes you need to make as you go.

- Being able to see you are moving towards your goal creates confidence. You CAN do this!
- Goals keep you on course and in action.
- Goals help you live a consciously created life, not a default one.
- Goals are motivational.
- Goals CREATE CHANGE!

Wow! Sounds awesome – so let's get into how you can create your own S.M.A.R.T.I.E goal.

What's a S.M.A.R.T.I.E goal? A goal that is specific, measureable, attainable, relevant, timely, inspiring and exciting!

At the beginning of the chapter we talked about my dreams of Bora Bora and Alaska. I was very clear that these are NOT goals. They are not goals as they do not tick all the boxes of a S.M.A.R.T.I.E goal.

Does yours?

Write out your goal and see if it matches ALL the following.

Specific

Are the specific reasons for achieving this goal clear? Why do you want to bring this goal into your reality?

Measureable
How will the achievement of this goal be measured? How will you know it's coming closer to you? How will you know when it's arrived?

Attainable
Do you have, or can you obtain, the necessary skills, attitude, drive, time or finance required to attain this goal?

Relevant
Is achieving this goal relevant to what you want or how you wish to live your life? How does it match your values? How will achieving it enhance your life?

Timely
Is your timeline realistic and flexible? Does it motivate you to take action?

Inspiring
Does this goal inspire you to take action towards it?

Exciting
Does the thought of achieving this goal excite you?

How did your goal match up? If you could not tick all the boxes, keep tweaking, adjusting and writing the goal out until you are satisfied it is a S.M.A.R.T.I.E goal.

Now we have our specific goal that is exciting and inspiring and timely. We are ready for it to leap into our reality. What next?

If this goal is quite large or is a goal that may take some time to arrive, you may be feeling a little overwhelmed right now. You may be feeling paralyzed. Firstly congratulations on having a HUGE VISION! Secondly, it's all okay – you just need to set some sub goals. Take a breath and come back to me and your note pad.

Consider what your sub goals may be. They may be yearly or monthly or weekly. Your goal is a place to come from, remember? Take some time and think about what the sub goals are that will bring you and your main goal together.

Write them out. Put them against the S.M.A.R.T.I.E framework. Work on each individual one until it ticks all the boxes.

Step 4: Consider potential obstacles

Did you think you were ready to set your actions? Not quite yet. Now we are going to consider the obstacles that may hinder our goal creation. This is the time to list all the potential obstacles or barriers that may prevent you from achieving your goal.

Some will be external situations you have no control over but I can guarantee that most will be within your control.

Those within your control include:

- Fear of failure, which often shows up as procrastination or perfectionism. Have you ever heard the saying "there's no such thing as failure – it's only feedback"? Thomas Edison told us he didn't fail; he just found 10,000 ways that won't work. If you receive feedback that the plan isn't working, adjust and keep moving.

- Not creating the time required. How can something new enter your reality if you don't create the time and space for it to appear? Take the time to create the time and welcome your goal into your life.

- Believing your inner doubter. It's very difficult to feel truly confident when creating something bigger, better or different than you have before. To keep the doubting voice to a whisper, ensure your action steps are as tiny as you can make them. If the voice is just too loud to ignore, seek help from a coach or counsellor.

- An unwillingness to embrace the pain. Many people want a washboard stomach, but they refuse to spend 4 hours per day in the gym. Some covert the CEO's role, but are not willing to commit to more years of study and 15 hour days in the office. Consider what you may have to sacrifice to achieve your goal and if you are prepared to do it. If you've honoured your values back when creating your S.M.A.R.T.I.E goal this shouldn't be an obstacle.

Step 5: Set Your Actions

The second final step in the process is to set your actions. These are the steps you'll take to bring your dream, now a goal, into your reality. Top tip – make the action steps as small as possible.

The smaller the steps are the easier they are to take. As you tick them off your list two AMAZING things are happening. Firstly, you have brought your goal closer to you and secondly you are increasing your confidence. Small steps for a big result.

Step 6: GO!

Don't wait. The time is now! Good luck!

Janelle Ryan

About the author

Janelle Ryan is a passionate and dedicated international Personal Coach, the founder of Sky High Coaching, a published author and engaging and inspirational speaker who credits everything that she's experienced in her life to date to her love and success in the life development arena. She was named one of Australia's Top Ten Female Entrepreneurs by My Entrepreneur Magazine in 2017.

Janelle's passionate and enthusiastic nature, along with her unwavering belief in her clients makes her a natural in working with successful high performers ready and committed to take their life to the next level. Her level of genius is her ability to use her intuition and skills in assessing what isn't being said and tapping into what is being communicated. She has a gift of seeing behind the facade and bringing forth her clients true inner most desires – even those they are not necessarily aware of themselves.

Janelle believes the path to a fulfilling and blissful life is not merely about goal setting and achievement. She believes underlying the pursuit of every goal is the need to make the change required – this change could be physical, mental, emotional or relational. Janelle works with her clients on clarifying their vision, busting through self-doubt, creating more confidence and living a life they want to live, rather than one they think they should be living.

As a natural working with others, Janelle finds that personal, private one-on-one coaching feeds her soul and she loves nothing more than the times she spends with clients from 3 to 12 months.

Her second love is experiencing the power a group of extraordinary people, working together, can create and she witnesses this via her boutique group coaching salons.

She believes everyone can take their life Sky High!

www.skyhighcoaching.com.au
Email janelle@skyhighcoaching.com.au
Like Sky High Coaching on Facebook
Connect with Janelle on LinkedIn

Success Is An Inside Job

Like you, I have heard some of the most incredible stories about people going from rock bottom to astounding levels of success. It almost seems as if prosperity is attracted to them and opportunity presents itself everywhere they go. How did they achieve this level of success in so many areas of their lives? Is success only meant for a chosen few who seem to miraculously defeat all the odds against them and rise to the top? Do you have to possess some superhuman ability that few people have or is there a much different story? Is there a blueprint one can follow to accomplish those ultimate goals and dreams they desire? In this chapter you will learn that many of the keys to success are not found in what you see, they are found beneath the surface.

Faith/Self-Belief

To build a life of continuous success, you must wholeheartedly believe in yourself and your abilities. One of the major things many successful people have in common is an unchanging belief in themselves. Michael Jordan, Elon Musk, Oprah Winfrey, and Richard Branson are just a few highly successful individuals who have reaped the rewards of a strong empowering self-belief. You won't be able to find an extremely successful person who does not possess a great level of confidence and belief in themselves. This belief is what motivates them to try again and again when they were knocked down or when they experienced adversity in the pursuit of their dreams. With this attitude and their willingness to take action no matter what, success would inevitably be the result of their hard work.

Their belief gave life to a vision so worthwhile that they didn't care how many times they failed along the way. They were determined to eventually get to where they needed to go.

On your journey towards success, it is a guarantee that you will experience your share of obstacles and setbacks. This rings especially true if you are an

Entrepreneur or Business Owner. It's all part of the process. However, if you have a strong belief in yourself and your purpose, you can tap into an incredible will to keep moving forward. Successful people get to the point that they do not allow anyone or anything else to get in the way of their dreams. If nobody else believes in their vision, they believe in themselves. When you believe in yourself, you don't need the approval of others because you are confident in your own self-worth. Having an undoubting self-belief that you have the potential to accomplish all of your goals is the starting point towards creating real success.

Vision

Desiring to achieve your goals is simply not enough to become successful. You must become a vision based thinker. Without a vision, your life is like a ship without a rudder and is in danger of drifting aimlessly. No empire, corporation, or brand was ever built without having a plan. In order to have a plan, it begins with an idea or a vision. If you are going to shoot for the stars and achieve those amazing goals you have, you have to become a visionary. The first step in accomplishing this mindset is to start thinking about the "you" in the future. Envision the best possible version of yourself, what you want to be like, and what you would like to be doing. Do this for your personal and professional life. This is all about the overall picture. Having this vision will give you clarity on determining what daily activity is required to make your dreams a reality.

You will then see what is in alignment with your goals and also learn what may be a waste of time. This is one advantage of having a vision because it guides you into making better decisions when it comes to your future. Any successful person will tell you that the majority of the actions they take are based on whether or not it will benefit them in the long term. Having a clear vision for your life will promote better choices in your daily life that will keep you on the path towards success. For example, a vision based thinker may exercise in the morning instead of hitting that snooze button on their alarm clock five times. Instead of working at a job they hate for the next 3 years, they will get out of their comfort zone and have enough courage to pursue something that brings them closer to their life long dreams. When you begin to pursue your goals with a clearly defined plan in place, you will see progress almost overnight. This is why having a vision is also an important piece of success.

Positive Self-Talk

Another thing successful people pay attention to is their self-talk. Believe it or not, every day we have a conversation with ourselves. Something as simple as spilling a drink or forgetting something may cause you to say "how stupid am I to do that" or "I am such an idiot". Ironically, if someone else were to say those same things to you it may hurt your feelings or stir up some anger. If that is the case, then why would we talk to ourselves the same way? Each negative statement we speak has the ability to get stored in our minds. There is power in spoken word.

Many people talk themselves out of success every day by saying things like "I'm not good enough", "I'm too old to be successful" or simply beginning with the words "I can't". Successful people know that this is a recipe for disaster and they instantly remove this kind of talk out of their vocabulary. Instead, they use words like "I have what it takes to succeed", "I am one step closer to my goals", and "I can". They treat themselves with the utmost respect, love, and encouragement.

They understand the power in the spoken word and are very careful in what they say to others and to themselves. This is why they use positive affirmations and empowering statements to maintain the right mindset. You must talk to yourself as if your only option is to win. "I will succeed" and "I am becoming great" are some examples of empowering affirmations that are spoken by some of the world's most successful people. It takes a great level of awareness to monitor your thoughts and words regularly. However, this is a routine you really want to put into practice. Words are seeds that can be planted in your subconscious and the wrong seeds can completely derail your opportunities for success. Your thoughts become things so remember to feed your mind and speech with positivity every day.

Focus

Focus is a major factor in becoming successful because it is the balance beam to all thinking. Without it, everything else falls apart. Your perception, your ability to learn, your reasoning skills, ability to solve problems and your decision making are all dependent on focus. It is impossible to maximize your potential in your personal or professional life when you are mentally unbalanced.

This leads to poor concentration on things that are important making you incapable of being productive towards your goals. Being constantly distracted will cause you to wander away from every assignment geared toward your success and place your attention on things that are a waste of time. Instead of taking advantage of an opportunity that will take your business to the next level, you are surfing social media, talking on the phone, reading emails, or binge watching the latest Netflix series. You must have good focus otherwise every aspect of your ability to think will pay the price. Having great focus will cause you to really look at where you are spending your time and identify everything that is going to keep you from the success you are working hard towards.

Additionally, successful people who are truly focused don't procrastinate. Of course they may be tempted to put off tasks that are overwhelming or unpleasant but then their discipline kicks in and they push themselves to do what needs to be done when it has to be. They know the best time to do something is right now and do not allow the temptation of putting thing off to distract them from what is more important. The ability to have laser focus on the right things will positively impact your life and business. It is without a doubt, essential to climb up the ladder of success.

Perseverance

Our world today is full of instant gratification, extreme multitasking, and short attention spans. It is because of this that we have really lost sight of a very important core element needed to take us to that next level of success. That element is persistence. The ability to keep going in the midst of adversity when your effort is met with setbacks or failure, is a real difference maker. If you take a look at any successful figure you will find that there was always a point on their journey where they had to give things another try. Sometimes they had to develop another skill, re adjust their strategy, or go back to the drawing board.

They understood that their success depended on their will to never give up and to do whatever it took to reach that level of greatness in their lives. Persistence does not take a college degree or a certification to obtain. It is one of life's greatest necessities and in my opinion, the most important component to becoming successful. I have met countless people with gifts and talents. The world will never know how great some of those people are because they did not have the burning desire to persist when obstacles arose in their lives.

On the other hand, I know people with far less natural talent but have achieved a level of success many dream about. These people have a level of persistence so high that nothing in this world could stop them from the pursuit of their goals. They also possess a great amount of self-confidence because they believe that they control their destiny. Persistence causes you to really take ownership of your aspirations. You own your goals, work hard towards them, and have an assurance that they will be achieved. This strong commitment to yourself and your goals is why persistence or "never giving" up is always eventually rewarded.

Gratitude

People who approach life with a strong sense of gratitude have a great awareness of what's wonderful in their life. They enjoy the fruits of their recent success and they continue to be prosperous. In the event things in their life don't go exactly as planned, they won't head for the hills. Instead, they always put failure or setbacks into perspective and seek to gain knowledge from the experience. Because they enjoy the fruits of their successes, they often seek out more success. It's almost like they have this pleasant aura around them and prosperity is attracted to them. When you begin to express gratitude and gratefulness in your life you will find that other people will want to be around you. Those business and personal connections you were trying to make will actually become drawn to you. I can't tell you how many life changing opportunities I have taken part in just because I consistently expressed a spirit of gratitude towards everyone around me. A spirit of gratitude will impact your character and your entire environment. Your mood will be pleasant, empowering, loving, and your confidence will be increased. It gives you a greater appreciation for life overall. You have to understand that success will not reward you if you are not thankful for what you already have.

The journey to success will become very challenging at times. However, you must always remember that there is something in your life that you can express gratitude for. In fact, living and breathing is a big enough reason to be thankful! There are lots of people who have missed out on life changing opportunities or valuable relationships because they were ungrateful. Make sure you don't fall into this trap. If you make sure to be grateful in all things, success won't be far behind.

Meiyoko Taylor

About the author

Meiyoko Taylor is a Best Selling Author, Entrepreneur, and Celebrity Personal Development Coach. For over a decade, he has worked with CEOs, executives, celebrities, public figures, industry leaders, & entrepreneurs. His mission is to help people recondition their inner world so they can achieve greatness in their life & business.

He is also a Certified Master Life & Emotional Mastery Coach, NLP Practitioner, and continues to work with the best and brightest in the leadership development field

With many years of success coaching, speaking, and most importantly, genuine, in-the-trenches business & life experience, his view is radically different. Meiyoko passionately shares with his listeners that success and leadership is built from the inside out. It is not about title, tenure or position. The opportunity for breakthrough success in every area is for everyone, every day. It's how we should all live our life. However, everybody's version of success is not the same which is something Mr. Taylor understands.

Taylor, sometimes referred to as the "Trajectory Changer" for his ability to re-connect people to their passion and life-long goals or as the "Big Brother Coach" for his coaching skill that brings out the best in people through a loving, practical, street-savvy style.

Meiyoko fusion of real-life stories, and his conversational techniques connects his audience to an intimate, intense and individual level of self-discovery.

Contact

Twitter @MeiyokoTaylor
Instagram @MeiyokoTaylor
Facebook @OfficialMeiyokoTaylor
Website www.meiyokotaylor.com
Email meiyoko@meiyokotaylor.com

Develop A Successful and Resilient Mindset

Walt Disney said, "All our dreams can come true, if we have the courage to pursue them." What separates those who merely dream from those who achieve their dreams? What gives us the courage to pursue what we want most? What keeps us going when we are confronted by obstacles and people who tell us our dreams are impossible?

The answer is the same whether you are talking about winning the Super Bowl, taking your company to the Fortune 500, carving a masterpiece like Michelangelo's David, writing a book, losing weight, getting a promotion, being a good parent, or enjoying a happy marriage. With the right mindset you can be successful at anything.

What exactly is mindset? Mindset is a broad term that describes ones beliefs. No one has exactly the same mindset because different upbringing, experiences, and interpretations of the world create our beliefs. The creation of beliefs is done automatically as we live and the majority of them are established by the age of six. Our minds automatically attempt to make sense of our world, and we use generalizations to do so. When a concept seems to adequately explain an experience, the young mind attempts to use the same concept to explain other situations. If the concept works, repetition causes it to become a belief.

Our established beliefs can help us succeed or they can hold us back. Once a belief is created, the mind begins interpreting reality as if the belief is true. It does not matter if the belief is true or not. The mind interprets reality as if it is.

Once we unconsciously develop beliefs about the world it is difficult to perceive the world outside our beliefs. Our senses bring millions of bits of information to our unconscious mind at any given time. The conscious mind receives only a tiny fraction of the information our unconscious mind can access. The information we become consciously aware of depends on our beliefs. Information that supports our beliefs is passed to the conscious mind, but information that contradicts our beliefs is not passed along.

For example, information about jobs that would be easy will not make it through the filters between the unconscious and conscious mind of someone who believes "You have to work hard to get ahead." Yes, many people have to work hard to get ahead. But there are exceptions—evinced by those people who seem to be lucky or blessed for whom everything just seems to come easy. Instead of looking at lucky people and asking ourselves what they do that we aren't doing, we resent their success. If there are exceptions to the belief, it is a belief that you can change.

Our mindset impacts our ability to be successful because the opportunities we perceive are either limited or expanded by our beliefs.

Changes at the level of mindset make changes to perceived identity, emotional state, capabilities, and behavior much easier.

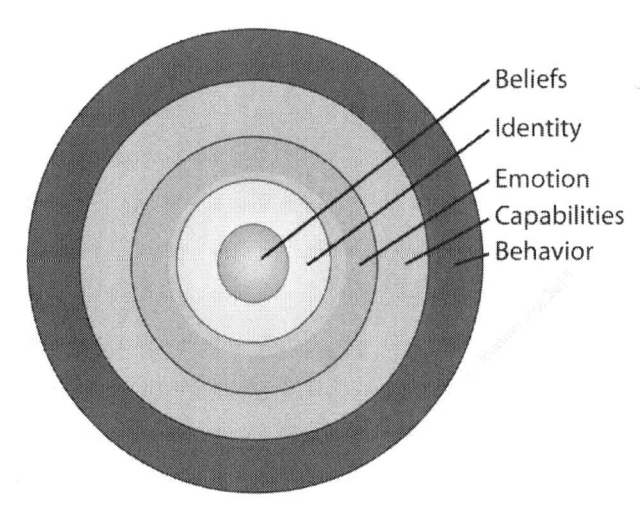

Beliefs
Identity
Emotion
Capabilities
Behavior

- Changes at inner levels affect every larger layer.
- Changing outer levels without changing inner layers creates conflict that the inner layer will eventually win.
- Permanent changes must be made at the inner levels.

Career and Mindset

Consider someone who has a low opinion of her chances for career success. The reason she has the low opinion is not important. There are many reasons she could have developed such a belief. She could believe that women face too much discrimination for her to achieve lofty goals or it could be more personal, believing that she lacks what it takes to be successful. I've worked with women who self-select themselves out of the running for better positions by not applying. When asked, they respond by stating it was a waste of time to apply when they know they would not be chosen.

Even in companies where females hold high-level positions, a woman who does not believe she has a chance does not try.

Likewise, a man whose Father repeatedly told him he was a loser may not believe he can be successful. The Father's expectation becomes a self-fulfilling prophesy, not because he was right, but because the son has accepted his father's view of his potential and his mind obediently interprets his opportunities in ways that agree with his established belief. When he has good ideas he will talk himself out of pursuing them. When he later sees someone else who was successful with an idea he talked himself out of, he will interpret the fact that he did not pursue the idea as proof his father's estimation was right—that he is a failure. But the truth is far different; the truth is that his action followed his belief that he was a failure. If he thought he was capable of following through on an idea and making a success out of it, his actions would have been different. His belief stopped him, not his potential.

Education and Mindset

Mindset also affects whether or not someone tries hard in school or gives up when a task is difficult. The belief that one is capable of learning, that learning is in fact a normal process that we continue to do throughout life, leads to persistence and the setting of higher educational goals. The belief that our intelligence is fixed and that our actions cannot change our level of intelligence causes many children and adults to achieve far less than their potential.

The truth is we can expand our level of intelligence. One of the world's most famous geniuses, Albert Einstein, explained it well, "I have no special talent. I am only passionately curious." Many people will consider anyone who passionately explores a complicated subject with curiosity over an extended period to be a genius in that subject.

Beliefs about the high cost of education prevent some people from attempting to find a way to go to college. Those who believe they can find a way, do so. The individual who does not believe he can afford college will not take the steps to find a way.

Relationships and Mindset

Relationships die all the time because underlying beliefs sabotage the relationship.

The man who does not trust his lady to be faithful drives her away, not because she did not love him or want to be faithful, but because when someone does not trust us, we do not feel loved. The woman who expects her husband to be unfaithful is constantly vigilant and questions him, allowing her lack of trust to erode the relationship.

When I help couples, I am continually amazed at the frequency with which couples that want the relationship to work allow fear of it not working to interfere with the love they could be enjoying. Disagreements and hurt feelings arise when words and actions are interpreted from the mindset that one has to be on guard. Every comment and action can be interpreted in many different ways. People who believe the first thought they think about the words or actions often misinterpret the intent.

For example, when a wife asks her husband what time he will be home, he may suspect she wants to hide something when she simply wants to have dinner ready for him when he arrives. Or she may want to be sure to end her own workday at a time that will allow her to maximize their time together. If he believes his wife is likely to be unfaithful, the lens through which he views her comment will not nurture the relationship. If he believes she has the best interest of their relationship as a top priority, her question will be interpreted quite differently.

The best mindset you can develop to foster long-term loving relationships is to trust that those you love have good intentions. A mindset that allows you to interpret their words and actions with the best possible meaning supports strong relationships. This is not the same as wearing rose colored glasses. If there is abuse or other unacceptable behavior, staying because you're giving them a 2nd, 3rd, or 50th chance is not good for you. You deserve better than that. But stopping yourself when you interpret their words or actions in a way that does not feel good and asking if there is a better-feeling way to interpret the situation will help you find perspectives that nurture loving feelings.

Health and Mindset

The power of the mind is amply demonstrated in our health and the biochemistry of our bodies. The Placebo Effect is the name given to a situation where someone believes something (most often an inert sugar pill) is medicine that will help a condition that ails them. The belief that the medicine will help leads to improvements that cannot be explained by the treatment received.

The Nocebo Effect is the opposite of the Placebo Effect. It is a belief that something bad will happen that then occurs, with no explanation other than the belief that it would. There are cases of Nocebo Effect causing death following a terminal diagnosis, where the subsequent autopsy reveals there was nothing physically wrong with the individual.

In a recent study, 74 students were exposed to an elevation of 3500' with some being told that the altitude could cause severe headache and the control group not being given that information. Only 20 of 38 students in the control group experienced a headache but 31 of the 36 in the Nocebo group experienced headache. The biochemistry markers including Salvitory cortisol (a measurement of stress) were also significantly more severe in the Nocebo group.

In a meta-analysis of 41 separate clinical trials, 64.7% of over 3500 patients treated with Placebo reported adverse side effects from the Placebo and 8.8% discontinued the Placebo treatment as a result of intolerable side effects. Individuals given saline solution but told it was chemotherapy have subsequently experienced nausea and hair loss.

Individuals who expect to die or experience complications from surgery have worse outcomes than those who expect a good outcome. One nurse I visited with who routinely worked with patients just prior to and following surgery expressed the wish that she could insist the most fearful patients' surgeries be delayed because they always had the worst outcomes.

The mind-body connection is real. If you doubt it, remember a time when you were nervous—maybe when the cute classmate or co-worker that you liked talked to you for the first time. Did you perspire? Did your palms sweat? That is just one example of the mind-body connection.

Researchers demonstrate the mind-body connection in countless ways. In one study, Salvitory cortisol measured before and after volunteers were told they would have to speak on a stage showed a marked increase. Just the thought of having to speak in public increased measurable stress in the body, clear evidence that what the mind does impacts the body.

Stress is the leading cause of illness and disease. Researchers credit stress as the underlying cause of illness and disease 67-100% of the time.

Stress causes a chain reaction in the body, leading to immediate decreases in immune function, cognitive function, digestive function and changes to the central nervous system. The immune system decline increases the risk of illness and disease. The impact of stress lowers the ability of the body to heal itself. Stress also causes adverse genetic changes.

Decreased cognitive function has been traced to decreases in pro-health behaviors such as exercise, healthy food choices, and avoidance of alcohol, drugs, and tobacco. It can also contribute to higher levels of risky behavior such as someone who speeds or drives with less caution when angry or upset.

Another long-term negative consequence attributable to chronic stress is pre-term birth. Although researchers do not fully understand the biological/physiological mechanism through which it works, chronic stress is believed to interfere with the biological time clock that determine the timing of birth, leading to an increased risk of pre-term birth.

The ability to self-soothe oneself from stressful perspectives leads to lower levels of stress, with both immediate and long-term benefits.

The term chronic stress makes it sound out of the ordinary but most modern humans are chronically stressed to some extent. The amount of stress we are willing to tolerate before taking action to reduce stress is far higher than what it should be.

Today, if you watch television, you are bombarded with messages about illnesses and other problems in a way that increases your expectation of experiencing problems—the commercials (i.e. erectile dysfunction and menopause problems) create a Nocebo Effect. Commercials and news reports often prime your mind to expect unwanted outcomes.

Recognizing the wisdom and healing abilities of your body and consciously reinforcing these beliefs can act like a Placebo.

Mental and Emotional Well-being and Mindset

More and more often, research supports the idea that all mental and emotional issues begin with stress. Strong and rapidly growing research support this conclusion, whether the problem is depression (which affects 10% of the population each year) or psychosis or other mental or emotional illness.

Worldwide, about 800,000 people die from suicide each year and attempted suicides are around 20 million each year.

Whether it is from loss of life or a life lived with less joy than is possible, the price we pay for tolerating stress is indeed high.

Happiness and Mindset

Stress is the result of mindset more than of circumstances.

When studying both happiness and stress, it quickly becomes obvious that they are two ends of the same stick. The lower the stress level someone is experiencing, the more happiness the person is experiencing. As stress rises, happiness (mood) decreases.

To improve one's level of stress, it is easier to focus on a desire to feel good and achieve better feeling emotional states than it is to focus on what is not wanted (high stress levels). It is actually possible to increase stress by considering how much stress one is enduring.

The best way to increase happiness and reduce stress is to learn skills so that even when stressful situations are encountered, confidence that one can proactively address and reduce the stress remains. Stress that one knows she can reduce is far less stressful than stress with an indefinite ending.

In the military, one of the tests they use to determine if someone will be considered for Special Forces is a run (with full gear on). The test is not about physical endurance. The candidates are not told how long the run is. They are simply told to run. They have no idea if the run is a sprint or a marathon. Those who can psychologically handle the uncertainty remain under consideration for Special Forces. The inability to handle the uncertainty eliminates many candidates.

Think about a time when you were under severe stress and how much better you felt once you knew there would be an ending to the stress. When my first husband decided he wanted a girlfriend and a wife but kept changing his mind almost daily between staying with me and leaving for his girlfriend, the uncertainty was almost more than I could bear. Realizing that although I could not make him stay, I could make him go brought such relief. It was not what I wanted at the time, but making the decision to end my marriage was less painful than not knowing what would happen.

Just by changing awareness of the outcome, my stress level decreased greatly and I was once again able to feel I was a fully functioning adult.

Prosperity and Mindset

Earlier in this chapter, you learned that beliefs affect your ability to perceive opportunities and that stress reduces cognitive ability. Working together, these two aspects of mindset cause those with more negatively focused mindsets to achieve lower levels of success. Mindset matters. The most convincing research comes from The Harvard Grant Study. The study collected data on 268 Harvard students and followed them for 75 years.

The students who had optimistic mindsets achieved the type of success one expects from someone with the advantages a Harvard diploma confers and included President John F. Kennedy. The more pessimistic students did not achieve the level of success one would expect and included more divorces, alcoholism, bankruptcies, and even suicide.

In the area of prosperity, I separate mindsets into a Lack Mentality and a Prosperity Consciousness. The individual with a Lack Mentality finds excuses for not pursuing dreams and goals. Lack of time, money, skills, resources, connections, education, and family obligations are frequently cited as the reasons they can't achieve. They accept these excuses as valid reasons not to pursue their goals.

Someone with a Prosperity Consciousness in the same circumstances expects to find a way to achieve his goals. The belief that he will find a way changes the filters the mind uses and allows him to consciously recognize opportunities. There are many individuals who have faced every type of obstacle that those with a Lack Mentality use as an excuse not to try who have succeeded, because they believed they could find a way.

How to Change Your Mindset and Beliefs

Changing your mindset and beliefs is easier than you might think. A belief is just a thought you accept as true and think repeatedly.

Beliefs are habits of thought and if you know how to change them, they are the easiest habits to change. The inner levels affect the outer levels. One common example is individuals who lose significant amounts of weight but still believe they are overweight. They quickly regain the lost weight because the belief affects the mind-body connection. The body obediently stores fat and the behaviors that stem from the belief encourage a return to a body image that matches the belief about the body.

Instead of Quitting, Become

A college professor who thought requiring homework that literally consumed entire weekends led my husband to ask me why I did not just drop the class. It was an enlightening situation when I realized that I had never once considered dropping the non-essential course. As a child, I was taught not to be a quitter. I was a Camp Fire Girl and part of our motto, which I dutifully memorized, was "I shall finish what I have begun." Shortly afterwards, I applied that new knowledge to my thwarted efforts to quit smoking. Realizing I was not a quitter, I decided to become a non-smoker. I was able to establish a belief that as of a certain date I would be a non-smoker and when that date arrived I went from being a 2-pack a day Marlboro girl to a non-smoker. I can't quit being something, but I can become something different, so can you.

Find Exceptions

It is easier to cultivate the belief within yourself that exceptions mean the belief is only true for individuals who believe it than it is to go on a search and destroy mission to find and stop believing things that are not serving you.

Reinforce Beliefs That Serve You

Begin thinking the thought you want to believe and reinforcing it. For example, at one time I believed all the good men were taken. When I recognized that this belief was the reason I was only meeting men I was not interested in, I shifted it slightly. I did not try to believe the world was full of good men who were available. Instead, I reinforced something I already believed—that sometimes wives of good men did not recognize what they had and left and sometimes wives of good men die and these situations create brief windows of time when good men are available. I also reinforced that it was possible for me to meet one during this window of opportunity.

After shifting my focus and making a belief that good men are sometimes available more dominant, the men showing up in my life seemed to change overnight. I met more good men in a month than I'd met in 15 years. That helped me further refine what I wanted so that very quickly I believed it was possible to meet what I referred to as my Mr. Wonderful, defined as the perfect man for me. Not long after that belief shift, I met my husband. He was literally in my backyard golfing with a friend. I now fully recognize that there were always a lot of good men but because I did not believe I could find one, I couldn't.

This exact same process can be applied to finding a fantastic job or business opportunity. With the right mindset it seems as if the things you want come easily to you. With the wrong mindset it seems they do not even exist.

Make it Believable to You (Take Baby Steps)

When you're changing a belief it is very important not to reach too far. If I had initially reached for the belief I now have about men (that there are good ones all over the place), my thoughts would have argued against the belief I wanted to establish because it differed so much from what I had experienced up to that point in my life. That internal arguing would have reinforced the belief I wanted to change, slowing (or halting) my progress.

Baby steps in shifting thoughts are best and they really add up quickly. By taking baby steps that you can actually believe, the evidence of the new belief shows up fast. Once that happens, it is easy to take the next baby step.

More General Thoughts

One way to find slightly better thoughts is to find general concepts about the topic. Negative beliefs are usually very specific. By shifting to more general ideas, it is easier to find a more positive thought you can believe.

Let's say, for example, that you are a teacher and believe that teaching and making a good income are mutually exclusive. This is the experience of most teachers and I've had countless teachers tell me that they love to teach but it does not pay well. One of the best things you can do to counter a strong belief is to find an exception. Teach yourself that exceptions are not special people with more talent or some special ingredient that you lack. They aren't. Exceptions are usually people who have stumbled into the right mindset. Some of them have done it on purpose as you're learning to do, but most were not as conscious about it.

Are there any teachers who are well compensated? Is there a way to teach and make a good income? Yes. Ron L. Clark, Jr. is an example of a teacher who found a way to help children and make a good income. He wrote a book and a movie was made about how his techniques helped inner city children exceed expectations. A mantra of If he can do it, I can do it might be helpful to you. Other people aren't better or worse than you are. They simply have different experiences, perspectives and have made different choices.

Recognizing that some teachers make a good (or better than good) income allows you to find general thoughts like:

- Some teachers make a good living

- Maybe I can find a way to be a teacher and make a good living

- Being a teacher does not mandate a low income

Reinforce the general and more positive beliefs about teachers' ability to earn a good income to change the filters your mind uses to decide which opportunities to pass to your conscious mind.

The same process can be applied to any negative belief.

Understand and Trust Your Emotions

Generally, our society values the brain more than emotions. The reason the brain seems to provide better results is because we do not understand how to accurately interpret emotions.

An emotion that feels bad (i.e. worry) is not indicating that the thought that caused the emotional response is valid.

Emotions are a comparison between your best potential and the way you're currently thinking. For example, let's say your child is driving herself to school for the first time and you're feeling worried about her safety. The emotional pain (an indicator of stress) from the worry represents the difference between the best potential (she has learned how to drive well, she will be cautious and be safe) compared to the thoughts you are thinking that are worrisome (she could have an accident, she might be reckless, she could be hurt, etc.).

The purpose of emotions is to provide guidance toward thoughts that serve us better. The concept is really simple, thoughts that feel better are leading us toward our highest potential self-actualized self and thoughts that feel worse are not on the straightest path to our best potential self. The worse the thought feels, the further the thought is from where you want to be.

Because we are taught so many things that contradict this understanding most people want to discard this concept or argue with it. I don't ask anyone to accept it just because I tell them this is the way it is. Instead, I ask them to experiment in the privacy of their own mind with different thoughts about situations in their life - and feel their own power to change *how* they feel simply by shifting their thoughts about the experience. Try it, you'll like it.

Give Up Excuses

The shift in mindset from a Lack Mentality to Prosperity Consciousness begins with no longer accepting excuses. Simply making a decision that you will find a way changes the potentials your conscious mind is aware of. You don't have to take a big leap of faith or figure out exactly how, you simply have to open the door in your own mind to the possibility that you can. As long as you believe you can't, you can't.

Believe in Good Intentions (Give others the benefit of the doubt)

I recently read a book in which the following advice was given by a woman's new mother-in-law, "The Lord will direct your way, if you let Him. You just have to believe. In God. In love. In each other."

You don't have to believe in God to see that when you consider this advice, it is easy to recognize that most marital problems are rooted in a lack of belief in love as a force with power of its own to bind and to heal, in the partner or self, or in a world where good things can last. Interpreting a spouse's words as hurtful means the interpreter believes the spouse would deliberately chose to hurt her, instead of giving the benefit of the doubt. Rather than being hurt when a loved one says something that initially feels hurtful, remain calm and question the intent behind the words. Most of the time, the intent of the words is to uplift or assist, not to harm.

Use your new understanding of emotions to help you give others the benefit of the doubt. Does doing so feel better to you? Try to find other perspectives from which to perceive the words.

Care Less about What Others Think

This may sound selfish and thoughtless but when you understand more fully why others think what they think, it is the only path that makes sense.

What anyone thinks at any given moment is far more a function of how they feel in that moment than the truth of that moment. A husband could come home to a sexy wife and a beautifully prepared meal, but if he had a bad day and is in a low emotional state he may respond by complaining about how much she spent on the steak she prepared for him. When someone is far from a state of appreciation they do not appreciate things that are easy to appreciate.

When it comes to your dreams, especially in the early stages, no one else can feel the powerful draw they have over you or how determined you are to succeed. Sharing dreams with others before your own confidence is steady and sure can lead to their doubts becoming your own.

In adolescent studies of resilience, those who reported low support from parents and teachers but high confidence in trusting their gut feelings and who had good self-esteem were among the most resilient. They were able to face their own problems and demonstrated an inner strength that supported them.

The Goal

The goal is not to ignore how you feel. It is to control it by changing your perspectives so that you are not as stressed. What you feel is what you feel. You cannot change how you feel without changing the perspective you have about the situation. You can, however, change the thoughts you think and feel differently. Emotions are guidance but what they are guiding you to must be understood for you to get full value from them. Pay attention to how you feel. Suppressing your emotions is the unhealthiest choice you can make and it ignores the guidance that can help you achieve your dreams.

Most importantly, be kind and supportive of yourself in your own mind. You must believe in yourself.

Jeanine Joy

About the author

Jeanine Joy is the Founder of Happiness 1st Institute (Happiness1st.com). With over twenty years of study on what makes humans thrive, she is a leading expert in helping individuals learn how to be more resilient, positively focused and optimistic.

She is a game changer focused on bringing better living to all with knowledge and practical skills she has woven together into programs designed to help individuals thrive more at all stages of life. Ms. Joy is a powerful author and inspiring motivational speaker, helping people achieve more of their potential.

Bibliography
(WHO), W. H. O., 2015. [Online]
Available at: http://www.who.int/mental_health/prevention/suicide/suicideprevent/en/
[Accessed 2015].
Ali, M. M., Dwyer, D. S., Vanner, E. A. & Lopez, A., 2010. Adolescent Propensity to Engage in Health Risky Behaviors: THe Role of Individual Resilience. International Journal of Environmental Research and Public Health, Volume 7, pp. 2161-2176.
Anon., n.d. Ron L. Clark Jr.. [Online]
Available at: https://en.wikipedia.org/wiki/Ron_Clark_(teacher)
[Accessed 2015].
Benedetti, Fabrizio; Durando, Jennifer; Vighetti, Sergio;, 2014. Nocebo and placebo modulation of hypobaric hypoxia headache involves the yclooxygenase-prostaglandins pathway. Pain, 14 7, Volume 155, pp. 921-928.
Dweck, C. S., 2008. Mindset: The New Psychology of Success. New York: Ballantine Books.
Peil, K. T., 2014. Emotion: The Self-regulatory Sense. Global Advances in Health and Medicine, pp. 80-108.
Stathis, P., Smpiliris, M., Konitsiotis, S. & itsikostas, D. D., 2013. Nocebo as a potential confounding factor in clinical trials for Parkinson's disease treatment: a meta-analysis. European Journal of Neurology, 12 November, 20(3), pp. 527-533.
Witthöft, M. & Rubin, J., 2013. Are media warnings about the adverse health effects of modern life self-fulfilling? An experimental study on idiopathic environmental intolerance attributed to electromagnetic fields (IEI-EMF).. Journal of Psychosomatic Research, 74(3), p. 206.

Voila
success.com

The best success books in the world

Beyond the Barriers to Success

"If we were talking to you on your first day here we would say, "Welcome to planet Earth. There is nothing that you cannot be or do or have. And your work here—your lifetime career—is to seek joy."
~ Abraham

Do you feel like the joyful success in your life is missing? Is it hidden from your perception and experience? Now is the time to reveal this missing element. Society has conditioned fears into all parts of our lives along with terms that stop our awareness of true triumph. Selfish has become the new meaning for self-care. Addiction was replaced with a new definition, abusing a substance. These all bring a new understanding to a word that originally told truth. Failure has become a word that produces shame.

Over time the meaning of many words are distorted and used against us. Is there really failure? This comment comes from judging another to make the speaker look good in comparison. Alternatively, it can make the other person feel less and unworthy. Telling someone that he or she is not successful, has become a way to reduce self-esteem, especially in the school system.

Thomas Alva Edison, who was an American inventor and businessperson, said that he was not a failure. He developed many devices that greatly influenced life around the world, including the phonograph, the motion picture camera, and a long-lasting, practical electric light bulb. "I haven't failed. I've just found 10,000 ways that don't work," he commented about his many attempts to invent the electric light bulb.

He seemed to be quite wise in life. He remarked, "Many of life's failures are people who did not realize how close they were to success when they gave up." Another of his comments is, "When you have exhausted all possibilities remember this: you haven't." Another observation by him about accomplishment is, "Opportunity is missed by most people, because it is dressed in overalls and looks like work."

What kind of work relates to success? Why does it delude you? This is the rest of the story.

There are two kinds of success. What others think of you in society can bring high acclaim, money and honors. Does it pump up your ego so you look good to others? Do you like the attention and acclaim? Is the limelight lifelong or is your 15 minutes of fame fleeting? Is social success brief or sustainable? Alternatively, does inner success bring eternal, lasting, and contentment that we call joy? Do you believe doing the right thing is never wrong no matter what others think? Is being comfortable in your own skin important? Is your self-esteem enough to validate yourself? Which explanation of success is yours?

I wanted validation, acceptance, and peace in my life, because my life was chaotic and dysfunctional from childhood and my marriage, I accomplished success as Valedictorian from high school. I soloed with a symphony on the flute. In addition to being the first in my family to graduate from college, I received the honor of cum laude. I always had high evaluations on my teaching ability over the many years I taught school. I looked like a success in my job, family, and community. However, I felt unwanted, lacked self-worth, and peace of mind.

I ultimately realized that personal fulfillment for success required me to apply new tools to my endeavors. My new tools became honesty, open-mindedness, and willingness. These opened the door to a new life where I could find inward achievement. I always paid my bills and never thought of myself as not being honest. I looked good to others; however, I lacked self-honesty. I had a clean house, taught school, belonged to the right organizations, took my children to their activities and never complained. Nevertheless, I was dying from poor medical protocol and my fearful state of mind. My insides and my outsides did not match. It was time to say, "I want a happy life and to feel good inside."

Becoming open-minded was another big challenge for me. My family was not open-minded. Growing up, I learned it was my stepfather's way or the highway. We looked good in church, but I was told what happens at home stays at home and what happens at church stays at church. The physical, mental, emotional, and spiritual abuse I endured was not discussed or ever addressed. Thirty years after I graduated from college, he mused, "We never got you a graduation gift, did we?" There were no opinions but his. He was the "God" of the family. I needed to be open-minded to a loving Heavenly Father, a Creator that would accept me the way I am.

The tricky one for me was willingness. I did not know how to begin with this one. However, I was told, "be willing, to be willing." That seemed to do the trick. Gradually, I found that Shakespeare was right, "The readiness is all". I was eager to give up my miserable life for a better one. I understand today, that life is about choice and free will. I could choose to align with a loving universal energy within and have better results.

I realized that fear in my life had stopped many successes. I became willing to release all the barriers to the love that was in my heart. Realizing and identifying that guilt, shame, anger, jealousy, and other negative feelings are forms of fear was a new understanding to me. They were obstacles to my achieving beyond my fear-based life. I discovered and released what was obscuring my accomplishments and achievements. I had been my worst enemy.

I preferred love to be my new motivation. I became willing to let love be my guide. Love is a choice. Over time, I came up with a new purpose. What is the most loving action for you and for me? This changed my consciousness from reacting as a victim bemoaning "poor me", into responding with considerate and thoughtful behaviors.

Because I was not acknowledged in my family for my achievements or worthiness, I did not give myself the honor I deserved. I was not only missing the acknowledgement from my parents, but I discounted and minimized my own successes. I did not see what I had achieved as worthwhile because I did not feel worthwhile.

I saw a movie called, "A Beautiful Mind" in 2001. It is an American biographical drama film based on the life of John Nash, a Nobel Laureate in Economics. He was diagnosed with mental illness. At the end of the film, his life seemed normal. When asked what happened, he replied, "I gave up listening to the voices in my head." It was time to change my voices in my mind to praise myself for actions and undertakings that were productive, helpful, and contributed to others. As I found my own self-esteem and became worthy, I was able to see my contributions and activities as genuine successes. In the past I had blocked my own successful feelings.

Edison was right it does take work. For thirty years, I have searched daily to identify and apply new life skills. These replace the old fearful ideas, behaviors and thoughts that were unconstructive. This has created a new foundation upon which to build my inner thriving mind-set. Through this search, I overcame my fears. It is an inside job.

Socrates said, "The unexamined life is not worth living." Over many years of self-searching, I found that my thinking was obscuring my inner truth of success with childish and selfish reactions from old disturbances. My motivations were self-seeking and my life was lacking love.

My success was buried deep inside under the painful trauma and drama of my growing up and destructive marriage. Surprisingly, today my outer successes are manifesting from my new inner understanding and knowledge that has brought balance and harmony. I feel successful today. Currently, my experiences are producing successful opportunities for which I did not plan or search. I am attracting new happy projects and activities that seem almost effortless at times. My heart became open to being a conduit of help and love to others.

Finally, realizing that the family's' rage was projected onto me and I was carrying their anger was a huge awakening. I shouldered their lack of success, too. Forgiveness releases us from the painful past. The people, places and events around you reflect the very parts of you that need mercy and love, so you can return to wholeness and joy.

Dr. Gerald Jampolsky states, "Forgiveness is letting go of all hopes for a better past." Your friends and enemies play a very important role for you, which you requested before this lifetime. You plan the events with your masters and guides before you incarnate. Accepting the circumstances you requested for your growth is important to releasing the emotional attachments. Sending love, gratitude, forgiveness, and compassion is the lesson that changes the energy you came to transform. Your loving response in each life incident restores your soul.

Do not be put off by the uncomfortable emotions that arise as you do this work, for it is merely the release of painful memories from the past now surfaced. You buried them deep in the subconscious parts of your mind. To do so was necessary to avoid going into deep depression or even despair when you were younger; however, they did expand and smolder within your memory. Now they can be released in their surfacing to leave. In healing, you see how you allowed them to inflate and grow over time.

The bridge between the duality in the material world and the oneness of a higher consciousness of love is forgiveness. I recently heard at a lecture a discussion about what is forgivable. The answer is - It is all forgivable. In spirit there are no actions that are too bad not to forgive. When I thanked those people in my meditations that caused me the most anguish in the past the energy changed. Immediately, I felt no influence from those old terrible times. I felt current and in the present moment.

In reality, all is viewed as equal in value, because otherwise is to see judgment. Therefore, all miracles are also equal without one being bigger than another is. It is, what it is, has become a familiar saying. "As forgiveness allows love to return to my awareness, I will see a world of peace and safety and joy." Course in Miracles, W 89

It is important to forgive yourself for putting yourself through such horrible criticism and condemnations from others as real. In A Course in Miracles, it states, "God gave the Holy Spirit to you, and gave Him the mission to remove all doubt and every trace of guilt that His dear Son has laid upon himself. It is impossible that this mission fail." T.82

Releasing the judgment of yourself and others allows space for learning love, faith, and trust. Understand that your thinking created the emotional reactions from fear. They were all based in illusion. When you realize that only what God creates is Real, and your thinking is an illusion, it is easy to release the old emotional ties. They dissipate into the ethers.

Your new understanding from this elevated realization and application brings feelings of caring and compassion. Without them, you would not be the new person today that you are. "No one is where he is by accident and chance plays no part in God's plan." The Course in Miracles, M. 25.

You are in the audience as the curtain now falls on the end of your play. Pretend others are on a stage in front of you. You stand and applaud vigorously. Bravo! They played their parts so well that you believed it completely. The illusion is over. You now see beyond the performance into spirit. You can see the love in their hearts beyond the parts they played for you to change. It becomes time to empower yourself instead of staying the victim.

With further understanding, I found that I had created the lessons for my maturity and to heal my karma. Those people and circumstances played out the parts I requested to show me how to grow and heal. I thanked them in my vision and realized I had made it up. It was like a fantasy or dream and I can wake up. What my mind makes up is not real.

This new understanding brought a deeper insight to what was hidden in my life. My "inner light" was blocked by all the fear of societal conditioning with judgments, criticisms, and condemnations. I was looking at appearances and not beyond.

Success is opening the doors to my heart so that the inner light can manifest out as love, success, abundance, and peace. The fears were like clouds blocking my heritage and birthright. Courage to open the door to my heart is to embrace life and all its beauty. To embrace joyfully all parts of the wonderful and incredible me! I was always a success in the eyes of my Creator.

The release of these emotional memories offers unconditional love to those who caused them and to you, as well. This will bring you a welcome sense of peace as you start to feel the uplifting energies nudging you towards a feeling of success. Love heals all karma. Love glues your shattered soul's pieces back into its whole. With this shift into a compassionate completely open heart, you return to God-consciousness. You now see through the eyes of God, the eyes of love. It is all love. You see the good in everything!

My favorite song is The Impossible Dream. As Don Quixote says, "The mission of each true knight... his duty—nay, his privilege!" He sings about wanting to overcome the negative messages in his mind that obscured his success. This is not about agreeing with it, necessarily, but understanding how you summoned it and why it may have stung. Because, yeah, you did attract it, and it does not have to sting any more. You take responsibility for your whole life.

A daily saying sent out from "The Universe" on the internet stated, "The beginner scorns criticism. The wise soul carefully weighs it. And the Master says, "But, of course!"

Your Focus Changes

Joy becomes your consciousness, as fear no longer exists. Some people call this being reborn. "To be born again is to let the past go, and look without condemnation upon the present" is another quote from The Course in Miracles T.234. You are born again into a completely loving spirit that fills your inner life. You become unafraid. You are a channel of love and peace. You are a love giver instead of a love seeker.

Moving into living in the "Now" is the presence of God's grace called the Fifth Dimension. Healing your broken soul through love returns you to being a "Whole Spirit"; you truly are a holy spirit. We are all one in spirit, a beneficial energy that fills and surrounds all of us. All there is, is love.

No longer, do the past harms and fears or future worries direct your life; you are free from old emotional baggage by this point. You no longer have opinions, judgments or beliefs. You have a new freedom letting go of egocentric, selfish, and self-centered earlier
motives. Happiness fills the void left by undoing the ego's power. Love is left when releasing everything unloving. Successfully, self-esteem is restored and emotional security returns.

Your inward feelings become fulfillment, triumphant, and contentment. You have a sense of prosperity, abundance, and safety that all is well. Having enough, being satisfied, and feeling rich in spirit flowers. Loving emotions of stillness and serenity replace your inner emptiness. A smile comes to your face as you enjoy your newfound success of inner peace. Because your needs are met, you are able to see where you can be helpful to others.

This quantum leap moves you beyond the old paradigm of linear time. You do not see the other person as separate and to blame, but one with you in spirit. Releasing the emotional connections of resentment, guilt, or revenge allows the realization, that your brain created your false impressions; they were not real. This person agreed to help you with your lessons. Thanking them rather than separating from them as if they are the bad person, brings unity of spirit.

Quantum physics is about unity, so is the Fifth Dimension and beyond. You have grown past your old consciousness of separation. Your old reactions are not your first response, anymore. How can you lend a hand in your new forward action?

Revealing Love the Real Success

Society, medicine, and religions teach you to look without for your answers instead of seeing what is within, the real you. Rarely, do you find someone who is yearning for immortality who shuts his or her eyes to what is without to behold the inner Self. Yet, when the outer distractions and beliefs leave, knowing arrives and success is found. Your beneficent inner power called spirit is experienced. You see beyond appearances, the invisible becomes clear.

"Sometimes you walk into things, that, if you were paying attention, vibrationally, you would know right from the beginning that it wasn't what you are wanting. In most cases, your initial knee-jerk response was a pretty good indicator of how it was going to turn out later. The things that give most of you the most grief are those things that initially you had a feeling

response about, but then you talked yourself out of it for one reason or another."
~ Abraham

Love is the highest power in creation and underlying harmony of the Universe. It is the supreme law whereby you throw off the bonds of separateness and perceive the great spiritual unity in which we have our fundamental essence. Happiness is a function of releasing your wants and desires for "Thy Will Be Done". Accepting the love within produces happiness. You become a channel of love, the highest vibration. It moves into the highest realization labeled unconditional love, light, or God. You are successfully channeling love to yourself and those around you.

Letting go of self-defeating ways allows the spirit to grow in gentleness and clarity. Through love, you serve; which brings prosperity, abundance, and well-being, which is real success. These could be called the fruits of the spirit mentioned in Galatians 5:22-23 of the Bible. "But the fruit of the Spirit is love, joy, peace, longsuffering, gentleness, goodness, faith, meekness, temperance: against such there is no law." The spiritual connection between you and others becomes evident. You are effectively bearing the fruit of the spirit, which is love.

Attracting Success through Higher Vibrations

When studying Edgar Cayce, I first heard the principle, "Everything is vibratory" #195-54. It made sense to me in understanding God as spirit. Everything is a vibrating energy in different planes, including your thinking about illness, scarcity, and even relationships. Higher vibrating energy is in good health, abundance and loving relationships. The vibrations range from the very negative, fearful ways of thinking to the highest and truest. When you journey through all degrees, you reveal yourself and find God. For without passing through each and every stage of development there is not the correct vibration to become one with the creator. Edgar Cayce #900-16

To improve your environment, focus upon the best things currently around you until you flood your own vibrational patterns with thoughts of appreciation. Finally, start a gratitude list that you add to daily to keep your focus on thankfulness. You need to lift all self-imposed limitations - all limitations are self-imposed - and free yourself to receive wonderful things. With changed vibrations, you can then allow the new-and-improved conditions and circumstances to come into your experience.

Ask yourself, what do I want?" Take one of your wants and ask yourself the following questions: How will I change when I get this want? How will my life change when I get this? What do I see my life looking like when I get this want?

In the moment, with your new state of being vibrating your own unique vibration, with no agendas or planning, you create your new life by attracting like energies in perfect synchronicity and timing. No one can deny you or grant you anything. You attract your success by matching the vibration.

My inner self releases the blockages and obstacles in meditation along with other supportive help. In addition, applying alternative health methods raise my vibrations. A few hints to help raise vibrations are flower essences, acupuncture, and tuning forks. These break the blocks that are stopping the energy from flowing and rising for the ability to move into a higher dimensional mind-set. I move past my fears of the lower vibrations. By facing my fears, I became fearless. What a feeling! "For he, or she, that is without fear is free indeed." Edgar Cayce, #5439-1

A New Approach Brings Success

A few years ago, I had to replace my skylight. The contractor put in another style that was not attractive. He did not discuss this with me before he picked a different style. I was upset as it spoiled the view of the woods, clouds, and sky when looking out. I asked for it to be corrected with the same design of my original one. His bullying and lies were complicating the disagreement. In the past, I would have submitted to his controlling anger that resulted. I found it hard to stand up for myself in the past, especially to harassment.

I found out that it was possible to obtain the same model as my old one. Moreover, I discovered that there was no law that prohibited my having it.

In addition, I filed a complaint with a business bureau where he had a high rating. Ultimately, he put in the acceptable skylight. I had successfully stood up for what was right. Through staying in the facts of the situation, I was able to triumph in this dispute of his trying to manipulate a situation that was not acceptable to me. My not backing down was a huge success for me.

This occurrence was the opportunity for me to move beyond my past into a better path of standing up for myself. Successfully I came from strength instead of the old victim I had been for years. I found myself to be the pot of gold at the end of the rainbow. I was the genie in the lamp of Aladdin.

Recently, when I became fearless, I found a new understanding about myself. There was nothing wrong with me. I was never a mistake. My life was not in error. It is important to accept that everything in life is as if it is supposed to be. This brought real awareness into my life. People are right where they are supposed to be in their journey. Situations actually brought new perspectives to my life even when at the time they seemed overwhelming and devastating. New insights brought new clarity and victory to my life.

I have found a simple way for the genie inside to find the reality that is buried deep down inside of my soul. It is in applying three principles. The first one is knowing that the only power is God. You shall have no other gods before me; this means to keep your focus always on God, any other focus becomes a false god.

The second is to neutralize the emotions surrounding the person or event that is the focus. It is not harmful, hurtful, or destructive, but a "lesson" for you to identify the energy which needs to shift into love, compassion, forgiveness, and gratitude.

It becomes your lesson and mirror. The person's face could be anyone and the circumstances could be different; however, it is your energy reflecting back to you for change. Lastly, there is no good and evil, the devil, or any other power, because God did not create them. You made it up. You made them up in your mind. What God creates is Reality. What you create is nothingness.

The key to staying in reality is consistently to remind yourself throughout the day and night that you are in this special place. I am in joy, in gratitude and in the presence of God. This is Reality. This mindset creates grace. God's grace is sufficient. Enjoy this serenity and peace of mind wherever you are. You always have been a success. You will attract successes.

How Do I Experience My Hidden Happiness?

Maybe you have felt that happiness has eluded you. It was buried under the fearful past and unattainable for you. Knowing that it is always inside and your outer focus from fear is the only barrier to your achieving this delight is the secret to life and your feelings of success.

Happiness is the experience of joy, contentment, and well-being, combined with a sense that one's life is good, meaningful, successful and worthwhile. The feeling of happiness is achieved by following one's heart and doing what brings you joy. There are many ways to train the mind to achieve happiness. Choose loving thoughts, words, and actions in every situation you encounter throughout your day. The more you cultivate your inner knowing through love, compassion, and observation, the more you become a vibrant source of happiness that radiates outwardly to others.
It is in one's innermost essence of divine connection that joy and happiness naturally arise. Most people call this experience, God. Experiencing happiness is about looking deeply within to see which action brings true happiness and which to eliminate because of suffering. Life requires discipline and effort but when you are nourished by happiness, exercising discipline becomes a joyful action that brings you more calmness, clarity, contentment and insight. It is treasuring every moment of life.
You feel better and more of the things that you want will flow to you. No one is keeping score. Your tasks will never be all done. Realize that you will never have everything you want to satisfy you. This unfinished place is the best space that you can be. You are right on track, right on schedule.

The best is yet to come. Wellbeing is flowing to you. Everything is unfolding perfectly. Life is supposed to be fun. Have fun! Join me on this new highway as we grow into love's oneness with harmony, balance, and bliss. Success is no longer hidden!

This is the path of the masters. The masters stress the liberating impact of realizing this truth. To realize God, to know your true identity, to become enlightened is why we descended and now climb back up Jacob's Ladder of consciousness, the spiritual ascension. It is the goal that we seek. Master Beinsa Douno says, "When …you find God, you will find yourself as well. When you see God, you will see yourself. To see God and to see yourself – that is the most sacred moment in life. Man lives for that very moment".
It is in that sacred moment that the ego defers to the Father, leaving only Him. In that moment, form becomes formlessness and God meets God. This is true success.

Rev. Marilyn Redmond

About the author

Rev. Marilyn Redmond, BA, CHT, IBRT is an internationally winning writer, speaker, teacher, and consultant. Her first book is "Roses Have Thorns". Her latest book is "The Real Meaning of 2012, A New Paradigm Bringing Heaven to Earth". Her forth-coming book is, "Paradigm Busters". Marilyn's books and E-books are at Amazon.com/Marilyn-Redmond/e/B0069WIKDC. She has written over 100 articles for Groundreport.com. Her blog is http://marilynredmondbooks.blogspot.com.
In addition, Marilyn is a spiritual counselor and internationally board certified to do regression, and past life therapy. Also, she offers tarot/psychic readings and private channelings. She was in "Who's Who" for Professionals and Executives for her pioneering and innovative work in restoring traumatic lives, healing emotional causes of illness and releasing negative energy. Her understanding and wisdom of the human dilemma and the solutions are from her personal experience. It will work for you, too.

Her lectures, interviews, and "Channeling from Higher Realms" appear on You Tube.

https://www.youtube.com/results?search_query=marilyn+redmond&page=1

Her web site is angelicasgifts.com for her columns, radio shows, art, and TV appearance. She is available for speaking, interviews, seminars, and individual counseling.

Managing Stress Is My Key To Success

I had enjoyed a successful career in the tourism and cultural industries in Australia before launching my small coaching company in 2007. I then proceeded to juggle full time work with running a business before 'hitting the wall' which to be honest proved to be a blessing in disguise. Initially I called the wall menopause, because that was what made the most sense to me at the time, but I was to come to see that there was a lot more going on than that in due course. What I experienced at the beginning of 2014 was the loss of clarity in my thinking, the temperature of my body rising astronomically (AKA hot flushes), and bone numbing, sleep eliminating, wellbeing dousing STRESS. Working my way through this situation was probably the best thing I could have ever done in terms of the long term health of my business, and my life more generally.

Basically getting real and skilling myself up to manage stress with mindfulness, mindset management, and general self care, was the order of the day for me.

I'm going to take a bit of time to spell out what actually goes on in our body when we're stressed, before explaining what you can do to bring yourself back into equilibrium whenever stress threatens to knock you off balance. This is not a departure into woo woo territory in case you're worrying that that's what it might turn out to be. This is simple, practical life and death information that reaches much further than success in the career and business spheres. It extends to success in relationships, success in health, success in finances - you name it.

So stress is the state our body goes into when it senses we're in danger. All animals have a stress response. It's a perfect adaptation that enabled all of the species we share the planet with today to survive. The problem is that humans have developed a maladaptive relationship with stress. Basically, stress is to the body what global warming is to the planet. It switches off one part of our nervous system - the parasympathetic nervous system, and switches on another part - the sympathetic nervous system. In other words, our parasympathetic nervous system gets overridden when stress takes hold.

This is not a good thing because the parasympathetic nervous system is the one that creates the ideal conditions for our body to stay well, with routine activities like digestion, growth, and repair ticking over nicely. The parasympathetic nervous system enables us to go about our business with a slowed heart rate, lowered blood pressure, and a heightened sense of wellbeing and calm. It's our sympathetic nervous system that's in play when we're in a stressed out hyperactive state. It gives rise to the classic fight or flight scenario. It raises our blood sugar and heart rate, narrows our blood vessels, and activates our immune system, which enhances our clotting capacity and blunts our pain perception. Basically the sympathetic nervous system ensures that the heart madly pumps blood to the muscles in order to get energy to where it's needed as fast as possible in the event of an emergency. It does this by flooding the body with adrenaline which increases blood flow, and cortisol which increases the level of sugar in our blood.

The problem here is that the process that goes on to mobilise sugar for energy activates inflammation in our body, whilst at the same time the stress response also automatically switches off any non-essential activity that could drain the energy stores that are needed to survive the imminent danger it perceives we're in. These non-essential activities include things like digestion, growth, and reproduction. Of course there are obvious problems with this given the chronic levels of stress many people live with these days. It's no good for us at all to have energy diverted away from these processes indefinitely.

Ultimately there's a maladaptation at play here, because unlike animals who only activate the stress response when there's clear and present danger, humans not only switch the stress response on in relation to non-life threatening circumstances like misplacing our keys or whatever, but also in relation to thoughts, memories, and emotions.

When we consider what's actually happening in our body when we push the stress button, it's obvious that we need to get a handle on this if we want to live to a ripe old age and enjoy the journey in the best health possible, not to mention being able to run successful businesses, fulfilling careers, and whatever else we might be working on that takes focus and energy.

The fact of the matter is that too many of us lead the kind of stressful life that means we're chronically experiencing increased blood pressure, which leads to hypertension that sets us up for serious damage to our blood vessels. This damage includes the build up of plaque, which poses the risk of the plaques breaking off and travelling to our brain in the case of a stroke, or our heart in the case of a heart attack. The bottom line is that in addition to playing a major role in a number of debilitating conditions including depression and sleep deprivation, chronic stress also makes the control of blood sugar more difficult. Type 2 diabetes is the canary in the coal mine in terms of the modern western diet coupled with the levels of stress many of us live with.

There's also the fact that we operate from our brain's limbic system when we're stressed to consider here. The limbic system is all about reflexes and short-term survival. This is exactly where we need to be when we're in real danger, but it's not where we need to be when we're trying to access our brain's capacity for higher order thinking and executive decision-making. We need to be functioning from our prefrontal cortex to access all of the intellectual faculties that enable us to succeed in business, and in fact any area of our life that requires things like willpower, memory, and judgement. On the other hand, operating from our brain's limbic system which is all we can do when we're stressed, means that our ability to maintain a healthy perspective on things and solve problems as they emerge goes right out the window. This is the area that started to worry me most when I hit that wall I mentioned earlier. My lack of ability to think straight made things incredibly difficult for me in terms of my business in particular and my life in general. I couldn't seem to remember anything. And I certainly couldn't do the kind of strategic thinking and communicating that had been the key to my success in my coaching, management and consulting roles previously. It was terrible really - I felt like I was drowning.

Basically living with chronic stress is like swimming in a rip in the ocean. We're culturally programmed to value action and staying busy, but action in a rip equates to struggle, and the struggle will wear us out eventually. On the other hand, if we dive under all of the activity by breathing deeply and coming into the present moment, we'll sense a point where we can be still and feel into our core. That is the portal that will take us back to calmer waters and take us out of stress.

Eating in a way that supports our body, exercising, sleeping well, having a healthy mindset, and pausing between activities during the day, are the kinds of things that are going to predispose us to being calmer on a day to day basis. This was the kind of tough love I had to take on board myself when my stress spiralled out of control with menopause and what turned out to be burnout creating a perfect storm in terms of stress for me. I won't say a lot about these particular conditions here except to draw the line between the fact that menopause for me meant out of control stress and scrambled hormones that led to lack of sleep, lack of energy, and diminishing cognitive ability. There's a bit of an interesting chicken and egg question here to think about as well. Was I stressed because of the symptoms of menopause, or was my experience of menopause worse because of the level of stress I was living with?

The point is that I had to do something about this if I wanted to keep my business and my life afloat. So in addition to the lifestyle points I made above about diet, exercise, and sleep, I put myself through a structured mindset and mindfulness program that I later packaged together for my clients to use, because stress is something that always comes up sooner or later with clients who sign up with me to be coached around an area or areas in their life that they want to broker improvement in.

What follows are the foundational parts of a program I developed as I worked my way through my difficulties in 2014. I now offer this program to my clients, and you can easily adapt the basics of it for yourself as well. The first thing to say here is that the most precious thing that is always available to help us manage stress is our breath. When we're relaxed, we tend to breathe slowly and deeply, rather than taking the kind of quick shallow breaths we take when we're stressed. Deliberately making time to pause between activities and just breathing deeply will make an almost immediate difference to the quality of your life. Simply focusing on your breath and slowing it down sets up a feedback mechanism that tells your body and your mind that everything's okay. That way your body won't be on standby for an emergency with the sympathetic nervous system engaged or semi engaged all of the time.

Basically, you want to be cultivating as many self care and coping strategies as you can. Breathing mindfully, journaling, meditating, exercising, taking a long hot bath, talking concerns over with friends, are all examples of effective coping strategies that I urge you to nourish yourself with.

The other important core change you can make that will release the pressure you would otherwise feel, is to start what I call mindset management. Essentially, if you take control of your mindset rather than having it control you, you'll experience much more joy in your life, and much less stress. This is because much of our stress is actually caused by what's going on in our own head. Forget about being chased by a lion, and try feeling relaxed when you've got things like perfectionism, paranoia, and a tendency to catastrophize going on in the back of your mind, especially when you're trying to close a deal, or make a business presentation, or even just get some sleep at the end of a busy day.

Whenever I think about mindset I'm reminded of a quote from Albert Einstein. He said - 'Everybody is a genius. But if you judge a fish by it's ability to climb a tree, it will live its life believing that it is stupid.'

It seems to me that the confluence of the educational systems that most of us come through, the families most of us are brought up in, and more generally the world we live in, set us up to struggle with the kind of crazy reference points Einstein plays with here. The upside is that the ball is in our court in terms of deciding how we respond to the kinds of cultural/psychological undercurrents that we're likely to experience in one way or other as we move through our lives.

Taking the time to look under the hood and see what's going on in your mind on a day to day basis will go a long way to your being able to avoid wasting too much time on mindless thoughts and actions that can generate a lot of stress, and even spiral out of control into obsessions or addictions if the conditions are right.

The problem is that many of our mindless thoughts have a sting in the tail. The exercise at the end of this chapter invites you to unearth some of the negative beliefs that might be filtering the facts of your life in a way that only shines light on the ways in which you are not good enough. 'Not good enough' thinking or imposter syndrome as it sometimes manifests itself, is incredibly common. It's crazy really. I see clients who've achieved amazing things but still manage to worry about being 'found out'. It seems that being made to feel stupid is one of the biggest fears out there. What's more, it's being harboured by some of the smartest people I know.

The bottom line is that worrying about being a fish who can't climb a tree is an exercise in futility and license to be miserable. With effort and focus, I was able to swap that kind of license for one that cleared the way for me to be for the most part happy and well. The strategies around mindfulness and mindset management that I used as I was going through menopause and burnout, helped me to breathe life into my future, by working with rather than against the biological changes that menopause in particular and getting older in general was bringing about. Gaining an understanding of what was being played out on a psychological and emotional level enabled me to metaphorically and practically come up for air.

If you don't take the initiative to manage what goes on in your mind, you'll find that your mind manages you with its default programs. One of these default programs involves compulsively thinking. Another one adds in automatic negative thoughts that seem to spring up out of nowhere. 'Not good enough' thinking is a great example of this.

In addition to, or maybe because of the propensity of automatic negative thoughts to arise when we're stressed, many of us resort to blame, justification, and denial as a way to avoid dealing with hard truths that are keeping us stuck. These mind habits along with perfectionism are particularly limiting frameworks that can keep us cycling around our problems without making any ground in terms of transcending them. I love Brené Brown's work on shame and vulnerability. Her take on perfectionism is that rather than it driving us toward being better, it's actually just shame wearing a disguise that ultimately keeps us small. 'Not good enough' is the language of shame that leaves us feeling as if there's something horribly wrong with us at our core. And a tendency to generalise takes 'I'm not good enough' and turns it into 'I'll never be good enough' and 'I'm no good at anything'. Your power lies in catching yourself whenever you notice yourself doing this kind of thing, and deliberately rewriting the script.

Another thing that keeps us stuck is compulsively doing, rather than being. Being busy involves going here, going there, doing this and doing that. Never slowing down to feel, and to check in with our body to find out what's real. Starting to experience life on the level of feeling rather than the level of thinking was a real game changer for me. It became all about more pausing and feeling into my body for clues about what's really going on, and less thinking and running around all day - day in and day out.

As I said earlier, our mind plays a significant role in keeping us stressed. The body on the other hand inherently knows how to relax. Actually feeling into the body is an incredibly effective strategy for managing stress. Awareness of how you're positioned in terms of your ability to receive and understand the signals your body gives you on an ongoing basis is a launch pad for real growth and healing.

I invite you to pause now and take a bit of a snapshot of the tone of your current mindset. Remember to be mindful as you ask yourself the questions you're about to ask. You'll need to make a commitment to set some quality time aside where you won't be disturbed to work through them at a deep level, and set an intention to create a metaphorical soft place to fall if you need one. You can keep this soft place to fall handy as you move forward into a life that won't have you bumping into hard surfaces in your mind all of the time. So let's see what comes up when you ask yourself -

- Where am I applying perfectionism in my life?
- How do I feel about that aspect of my life right now?
- In what ways am I doing really well in this aspect of my life?
- In which other areas of my life am I doing really well?
- What do I say to myself when I've made a mistake?
- What's a more empowering thing I could say?
- What do I say to myself when I'm tired?
- What's a more compassionate thing I could say?
- How do I show my self respect?
- How else could I show myself respect?
- How easy or hard have I made it to feel good?
- What could I do to make it easier to feel good?
- When do I numb myself?
- How do I numb myself?
- What has numbing myself cost me so far in my life?
- What could I replace this behaviour with?
- How will I work toward cultivate more self compassion?

This is just a bit of food for thought to get you started. There is a plethora of other more structured mindset management tools that are available out there to help you to slow things down and re engage your sympathetic nervous system which will slowly but surely change your life forever. Changing your life in this way entails making a commitment to take responsibility. It means turning up and being real, especially when things get tough. You'll know things are getting tough when you find yourself reaching for food when you're not hungry, or alcohol, or the credit card, or whatever it is that you use to numb yourself when the pressure rises. Watch this play out with curiosity and compassion, and start working on disrupting these patterns by pausing and breathing deeply, and interrogating the thoughts and feelings that come up just before the urge to engage in your numbing or distracting behaviours overcomes you. If you can manage to put the smallest amount of time between the impulse and the response you'll be giving yourself a chance to turn things around in a profound way.

Start to notice also whenever you feel yourself shrinking. What I mean by that is whenever you become aware that you're deliberately doing something to try to blend into the background so that you won't be vulnerable to being seen for who you really are. When you feel this starting to happen I want you to deliberately ground yourself by standing up straight and feeling into your legs and your feet with your energy radiating right down into the core of the earth. And I want you to feel into the feeling of standing in your power.

It's much easier when you're physically sensing your power to lean into your vulnerability and stay true to yourself. Make no mistake about it. It takes a special kind of courage to stare down any tendency you might have developed over time to shrink and/or numb yourself whenever shame and vulnerability come up for you. It's in nobody's interest that you live a smaller life than you're meant to be living. Not living the kind of life you deserve will generate stress one way or other. It's worth asking yourself what the stories are that you tell yourself about not deserving to play big, and what place these stories have in your past vis a vis the way you see your future panning out.

After getting my stress under control and my mindset back in a more positive space, it was easy for me to see that on a practical level I was overcommitted. It was clear that the time had come for me to make a choice between the security of the full time job I was well passed my use by date on, and my coaching business that I loved to bits. I bet it's not hard for you to guess which one I chose. In my own way I was keeping myself small by hanging on to the job that spelled security for me. I can now see my way clear to going from strength to strength in my coaching and consulting business. Managing my stress and my mindset enabled me to finish my book - The Ultimate Menopause Makeover – and develop a number of exciting programs that my clients are giving me fantastic feedback about.

I want to commend you for reading this chapter. I know stress management is not the sexiest topic in the world, and I also know that just as there are those who can find a way to deny global warming, there are just as many who are good at denying the damage that's being done when we let stress run amuck in our life. The bottom line is that you will give yourself a decided advantage over your competitors if you manage your stress. It's as simple as that.

I wish you all the best.

Jane Turner

About the author

As well as being a gifted speaker, author and sought-after business consultant, Jane Turner is a Transpersonal Coach with Master Coaching qualifications through the Behavioural Coaching Institute. Jane is also a Neuro Linguistic Programming Master Practitioner, and holds Counselling for Health and Social Care qualifications through the Medical Register of Australia.

Jane has an extensive background in developing teams to deliver high level corporate results. This background augments her years of experience as a coach working with clients individually and in group settings to transform the results they are experiencing in any and every area of their life.

Jane works with people all over the world from her base in Sydney Australia where she lives with her husband and teenage daughter.

Her book "The Ultimate Menopause Makeover" was published in 2014. She now regularly runs her "Simplified Book Writing" workshops for others who want to write a book to boost their industry credibility and authority.

Success By Choice

What is success?

Act 1

Too many years ago to think about, I gained my first Management Consultancy contract for my solo entrepreneurial business.

I was excited. I had my freedom. I was doing what I loved.

I was proud to be contributing to workplaces where people were valued and the organisation was thriving, ethical, creative and humane. Before I knew it, I was getting assignments nationally and internationally and being asked to open conferences and speak as a keynote. I was doing innovative, groundbreaking work and getting paid well. Everything was great.

I was being successful!

My husband's career took off. He had become CEO of a government organisation. His work was demanding and time consuming.
We had a beautiful house, the kids were doing well in their private schools and then....

The cracks started to appear.

My husband and I worked well together, both of us were happy for each other, but, we were like ships passing in the night. We had 21 happy years, but we were now dis-connected from one another. I said at the time, "I love you, but I don't love you". I now know that was naive. I did not know how to resolve what I was feeling; at times inner tension and at other times, blandness. I was experiencing a dis-connect between my thoughts and my feelings, only I did not know it at that time.

We had an amicable divorce and I took time off to recuperate and take stock.

I had success at work AND success in my relationship until the things that had never been reconciled in my life surfaced to be reconciled. In Jungian terms, it is called our shadow. Anything from our past that was never resolved screams out to be resolved. I could not feel and sense the love and loyalty that was present in the relationship. I was like so many of us today, dis-connected.

Whilst, it was being busy that was a trigger for feeling alienated, the dis-connection between what I was thinking and what I was feeling, had occurred long ago in my childhood. We often mistake an issue in the present for something that is occurring now, when it is really inter-connected with our history. New events trigger old memories, the good ones and the ones that we have locked away. Learning to discern the difference between what is happening right now and what is a memory from a past event is critical for success. Projection of past issues on to current events leads to adversity and mis-understanding, not success.

As a baby boomer, I had bought the myth that success was having it all; work where you are paid well, respected and fulfilled; a happy family; an active member of society and community; physically healthy; perhaps an artist, musician or gardener and more. I am not alone. It is not only the baby boomers who strive for success and perfectionism, it is hot on the list of why young people today are committing suicide as they do not feel "good enough" or successful enough, compared to their peers.

We want success, but at what cost?

Do we need to re-think what is success?

The myth of perfectionism and having it all at once, is now being torn apart gradually by some. It is now a growing trend to plan a career pause for family.

"The youngest generations of women in the work force — the millennials, age 18 to early 30s — are defining career success differently and less linearly than previous generations of women."

It is with much delight that I hear about families choosing to re-define success today.

Act 2
My attempts to re-define success sent me on another journey the second time around. Now single, running my own business, caring for children between two homes and caring for a home on my own.

Have you experienced stopping after being extremely busy and you suddenly realise you are more stressed than you thought you were? I needed more time to chill out than I thought and I was not going to let work and being successful in business take me away from the things that mattered to me.

That is, until, another pull away from how to create success on my terms caused a major downturn in my life.

I entered into another relationship.

This time I was going to "make sure" the relationship was successful and I would successfully care for adolescent children, parents, friendships, my soul connection, creativity and my health. Whilst still wanting to be successful at work, I found the second relationship demanding, de-moralising and unsupportive. The more I gave, the more he wanted. It was never enough. I could not succeed in my work whilst being so drained from giving to a bottom less pit, which sucked the life from me, without receiving any sustenance from the relationship.

Success in Different Dis-guises
My success at this time was letting go of my second relationship when I accepted the misogynist, narcissistic behaviour was not love and resulted in my self-worth eroding. I had to accept my love for the part within him that I could see was good was not going to change him, as he would not take responsibility for his sadistic behaviour and there was nothing I could do to change him. Without self-belief and the freedom to make choices aligned with my truth I could not be successful in my personal or work life. Fortunately, I had the strength and conviction to know the relationship was abusive and I needed it to end to create a successful life.

Success of Another Kind
With aging parents who needed care there was no other choice for me but to take the time to honour their wish to age and die at home. My paid work was put on hold, whilst I self-funded a sabbatical to care for my parents.

Success was in getting to know my Mother newly as she aged, softening into a whole new relationship with her that resolved any historical conflicts and mis-understandings. Her greatest wish was to die in her own home, with her loved ones and the familiarity of place supporting her pass over with love, dignity and respect. Being with her as she aged and passed over, enriched me beyond words. I had been successful in her dying well.

There were many treasured experiences that I would have denied myself, if I had prioritised being successful in business over helping my parents die well.

Act 3

Free from family responsibilities with adult children who were creating their lives and my parents passed over, I was now free to create what success meant to me in the next stage of my life.

This time I had the intention of a deep re-consideration of what choices were aligned to my truth and my deepest values and would contribute to my success across both my personal and work life. The work I have done with the many people who I have been fortunate to Coach and Mentor has now culminated into a synthesis of strategies and skills so that I can guide others to connect to their own truth and find what success means to them in their own terms, at any stage of life. What I have come to know is that success is not fixed, or permanent. How we define success changes at the many different periods of our life. What is success today may not be tomorrow.

The Lessons I learnt About Success

Success is about making Powerful Choices in the pause between a stimulus and our response.

> "Between stimulus and response, there is a space. In that space is our power to choose our response. In our response lies our growth and our freedom."
>
> — Viktor E. Frankl

Being human we are blessed with the power to choose. We can make choices that are good for us and bad for others and the environment. We can make choices that are both good for others, our environment and ourselves.

When the pause is too long and we sit on the fence, we often do not think that is a choice, but going to and fro for too long limits the success we want to achieve, as we do not take actions towards our dreams. It is like being paralysed. I learnt how uncomfortable sitting on the fence is, when I stayed too long in the defacto-relationship that exhausted me and eroded my self-worth.

When the pause is too short or we rationalise our choices without being connected to our deep soulful connection we are likely to make choices that are not for our whole hearted success. When we are dis-connected from our sensory, emotional and spiritual body we are more likely to make choices that are not successful. We may lack compassion for ourselves, perhaps giving up our needs for others, or we may blindly be selfish and create our own success at the expense of others. Both of these ways I do not define as success.

One of the most important skills we can learn to create the success we desire is the skill of deep self-reflection in the moment that we pause.

Deep self-reflection includes accessing information from multiple sources; our physical state, our senses, feelings, thoughts, energy and memories. In artful and reciprocal conversation with those who we trust, we can learn the art of uncovering our blindness.

As David Abram, so beautifully writes, in "'Becoming Animal",

"A way of thinking enacted as much by the body as by the mind, informed by the humid air and the soil and the quality of our breathing, by the intensity of our contact with the other bodies that surround."

It is this kind of presence and self-reflection that reveals our blindness of what what we are doing to sabotage ourselves and what we are doing that is creating our success.

Throughout my mid-life journey I learnt to deepen my practice of self-reflection, learning the art of interpreting messages from my emotions, from sensing my energy and the physicality of my response to the environment, people and places. I learnt to re-connect to ancient wisdom stored within my body, in much the same way as the 'Wayfinders", the Polynesians who were sophisticated in their sensory and intuitive ability to successfully navigate the sea without instruments. There is a story that American Indians could not see the first sailing ship on the horizon when Columbus discovered America, as they had never experienced one before. We do not hear the story that Westerners could not see the intuitive intelligence these people were accessing as a way of life, as it was not in their experience. We are only just beginning to re-connect, see and accept the intelligence in more than our logical brain. The Polynesians had a practice of grounding themselves to the centre of their being, through their navel, and sensing the wind, water, stars and nature to intuit their path safely through treacherous waters and live their lives.

It is these sensory and intuitive skills that I have now developed which enable me to co-creating my world with a new definition of success.
It is these skills that shine the light on the "control" virus that inhabits us in more ways than we may imagine, when we wonder why we are not being successful.

Imagine for a moment that you are looking through a movie projector at a movie. Is all you can see is a movie made up of beliefs about having to be in control and dominate our world. Have you been acting as if you can control your world and as if your security comes from owning and controlling "things"?

Now, put another lense in the camera and see another picture. The second picture sees humans as inter-connected with each other and our natural environment. People are learning to adapt, to create, to be spontaneous, to respect the inter-dependence we have with each other and our environment.

This is the connection we can make. Connecting to more of the intelligence in our body, our senses, our intuition and the intelligence within the environment in which we are placed. Just as the Wayfarers learnt this intuitive language so can we. When we restore the connection between our thinking, logical brain and our sensing and intuiting intelligence we have the capacity to re-define success in ways that could not imagine.

I call the gap between thinking and feeling a dis-connection. In psychology this natural human phenomena, is called dis-association. Humans and animals dis-associate from our body and our emotions when under threat and to protect our-selves from harm. In animals, scientists believe the dis-associated state may be almost like creating amnesia, prior to the predator eating their prey.
In western society there is much advice about our reptilian brain generating fear as if it is not necessary today, as we do not have predators such as woolly mammoths waiting for us on every street corner. I think differently. We have predators of a different kind today. Predators who prey on the kindness and generosity of others and the attacks are psychological, financial, physical and emotional. I believe it is just as necessary today to understand that fear arises when we need to create safety. We need a different kind of safety than nomads or cave dwellers, but we still need to create our own safety.

If we are not attuned to sensing out predators today we can fall into sabotaging our success through our lack of sensory and intuitive abilities. Learning how to understand the messages from our senses and emotions from a young age enhances the success we can create over our lifetime.

If we have had to protect ourselves as children, and not learnt how to release the tension from defending ourselves the unresolved tension can manifest as control, bullying, meanness and self-sabotage later on as an adult. Is it any wonder the statistics for bullying in both the workplace and at home is significant when many people do not have the skills to resolve early defensive behaviours.

Fortunately, there are new interventions in schools teaching young children emotional skills, the ability to self-care and create boundaries of respect.

The dis-connect I am sharing with you, not only arises from being attacked at some time. There are a plethora of modern day technologies constantly pulls us out of our bodies and into being dis-connected from our emotions and visceral experience of being alive and human.

The prevailing use of technology is not going to go away and there are great benefits to society through our technological advances. Like anything when we become so addicted to it and lose sight of using it as a tool, not as a way of life, it can have adverse unintended consequences.

Another key pre-occupation that takes us out of our body is our obsession with rational thinking at the expense of sensing, feeling and intuiting information from within ourselves.

The last one to share in this chapter is an over reliance on seeking answers outside ourselves from experts.

These 4 elements dis-connect us from our humanity, wholeness and ultimately success.

1 Psychological and Physical Dis-association from Trauma

2 Technology and the Dis-connect

3 The Dis-connect arising from rational thinking at the expense of emotional and intuitive ways of thinking.

4 Over reliance on outside experts for our answers

I summarise this journey to intuit and sense my truth and success in the diagram below.

Journey to Success

Level	Trait	Success	Focus
Sage	Wisdom	10 x	Patterning
Leader/Follower	Intuition	8 x	Embodying
Leader	Creativity	7 x	Playing
Expert	Freedom	6 x	Voicing
Competent	Resilience	5 x	Sensing
Informed	Dis-Belief	4 x	Noticing
Novice	Overwhelm	2 x	Exforming
Starter	Perfectionism	1 x	Choosing

@deborahlange
www.deblange.com

This model is a visual representation of the focus I took and the development that I gained over time. I developed this model based on my experience. I applied the learning with different groups of people who came to me saying they were successful in one area of their life but not in another. Usually it was success in a technical competence and not as successful in personal relationships. The Model has been applied to men and women from different age groups. From Senior Executives who at the end of their careers wanted to learn how to lead people and with younger people who came to me, in their 30's saying, "I am successful in some areas of my life but not successful in others, what am I doing? I do not want to repeat habitual patterns or make the mistakes of my parents".

I share here a story of how Vanessa, a young woman who came to me for Mentorship, journeyed through the stages in the model above to reach new success in her life and work. Vanessa contacted me feeling stressed after a relationship break up and with challenges working for a boss who she found highly controlling and demanding.

Vanessa, recognised she was a perfectionist. She had to do things differently as she was constantly anxious and doubted her ability to create success in her life.

The Choice

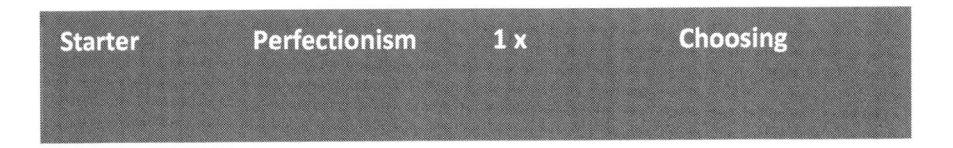

Starter	Perfectionism	1 x	Choosing

She paused, breathed and made the choice to self-reflect. There was a noticeable shift after our first session, when she made the choice to begin. She immediately began seeking new friendships rather than staying isolated and ashamed after her break up. Re-newed success in her personal life was beginning.

We are on the way to being more successful as soon as we choose to pause and consider what is happening deeply rather than continuing to react to life events. When we start we are 2 times more likely to choose a more successful response for the best interests of self and other.

Exformation

Novice	Overwhelm	2 x	Exforming

There is often a feeling of overwhelm when knowing you are at the beginning of an unknown journey. We have much information available in the world today and we are often full to the brim with emotional tension. Vanessa learnt to exform emotion that had been pent up and was blocking her feeling of happiness. She exformed thoughts through journaling and released emotion through giving herself permission to feel her fear, to cry, laugh and sing with joy.

Exformation increased her ability to create success in her life 3 x more than if she stayed tight with tension held within her body.

Noticing

| Informed | Dis-Belief | 4 x | Noticing |

Pausing and reflecting on how our actions are aligned with what we say or are not, reveals our truth and our blind spots. Vanessa revealed her childhood beliefs about having to be perfect to receive love from her parents. This led to her addiction to striving for success by being perfect and to never feeling good enough. She could not say no to her boss when he requested more work to be completed at any time. This resulted in working 80-hour weeks which was not good for her health and wellbeing. She was compelled to be the perfect partner, expecting nothing from a partner, whilst having to give the best of herself. When Vanessa revealed her blind spots and her false beliefs she learnt to say no and to create new boundaries of respect. Her behaviour influenced her boss. He began to walk along side with her and support her rather than driving her hard.

Sensing

| Competent | Resilience | 5 x | Sensing |

Vanessa was now learning to sense the difference between the energy of perfection and striving and the energy of flow and success with ease and grace. She learnt how to adapt to situations and became more resilient rather than being attached to the perfect answer to everything. Her success was growing incrementally.

Voicing

| Expert | Freedom | 6 x | Voicing |

Resilience gave Vanessa a new sense of freedom to speak her truth. This improved the success of her relationships with family members who constantly asked for her support. Previously she could not say no to family members requests for support, and gave her support to others leaving little or no time or resources for herself. This left her feeling spent. Now with the ability to voice her truth she increased the success in her relationships at work, with her family and with prospective new partners.

Playing

| Leader | Creativity | 7 x | Playing |

Vanessa now gained new respect from her peers and managers. She was asked to manage teams and she had the freedom and strong sense of self to be playful at work, to build relationships with intimacy and connection and to be creative in response to work place challenges. This was mirrored in her personal life. She began to choose new pursuits such as playing the drums, drawing and singing. She began to be more creative in designing her home as a sacred and beautiful space to nourish her self after work. Play and creativity was increasing Vanessa's success 7 x more than before she began this journey.

Embodying

Leader/Follower	Intuition	8 x	Embodying

Whilst developing these new skills, Vanessa became aware of a heightened sense of intuiting which people were controlling and energy drainers and which people were energising as they embodied values of respect and freedom similar to her own values. She was now embodying her own values of freedom and self respect and could let go of the need to control others. In turn she could sense easily when she was being "controlled" by others and could create new boundaries of self-respect. She began to discern better at how to spend her time and who were the tribe of people who she could be with at work and at home who appreciated each other's uniqueness. She was attracting different people into her life with ease and grace.

Patterning

Sage	Wisdom	10 x	Patterning

Vanessa now has the skills for life to be able to adapt and learn from life events by choosing to pause and deeply embody reflection. She can now apply her sophisticated suite of skills to discern a deeper dimension of what she is doing that is creating her success and what she is doing that is potential sabotage. She can reveal unconscious patterns in her own behaviour and in events and behaviour of others.

She has opened herself to the unseen, to what can be "intuited" through sensory and imaginary data, to new fields of possibility that have never been considered before. She is now 10 x more successful than when we met.

Vanessa's 2 year journey went;

From angst over divorce in her personal life, to knowing it was the right choice
From controlling, dominating parents who made her feel guilty, to an adult - adult relationship of respect
From hating being single, to loving herself and her life
From dating people who did not suit, to consciously sensing who had similar values to date
From dating the "wrong" people, to becoming exclusive with a new partner
From a marriage where there was dis-respect, to a new marriage which had solid foundations of trust, skills to resolve conflict, be loyal and a backbone to one another, with the realisations that both of them unintentionally triggered each others' weaknesses and it was the opportunity to strengthen themselves and grow into their best selves.
From a controlling boss, to a boss as a partner
From needing to stay in a Corporate job for security, to choosing to leave the Corporate life, and being asked back as a Consultant
From being unhappy and single, to creating a family and visioning a successful life with family and fulfilment in work

Her life was not going to be like this with the skills she had when she first came for Mentoring.

Some of her greatest fears were overcome:

"Will I repeat the mistakes of my parents? Will I ever be good enough to create successful relationships? Will I ever be good enough at work and not have to work 80 hours a week to prove myself? Will I be successful at work and home?"
Vanessa has re-defined success and has shifted from being a perfectionist and creating stress in her life to becoming successful at making wise choices in both her personal and work life.

In essence, she has become like a SENSEI, of personal mastery of sensory and intuitive capacities, being able to integrate the rationale with the intuitive for her success. She is able to:

- Sense and activate her multiple sensory capacities and integrate this with her rationale thinking

- Express her energy and emotional expression, exforming what is blocking her and creating the space for the new to emerge

- Notice blind spots, triggers, beliefs and uncover the congruence or incongruence of her actions, feelings and words

- Synthesise new information with playful improvisation that fosters freedom, connection and fulfilment

- Engage with self and other non-defensively to check that her new knowledge is taking her towards her vision and aligned with her values

- Intuit the unseen and be open to the emergence of new possibilities that rational logic does not allow

Vanessa, learnt these skills to be more successful at creating her life and at the same time, my life changed as well.

Act 3

In this third stage of my life, my boundaries between work and life are blurred in a way that is creative and nourishing. This time I am keeping the connection to my heart's desire with a whole new sense of myself, relationships, life and what is important to me and my valued clients.

I feel deeply present in my body; I connect to nature and my spiritual guidance as a daily practise. I am not following some-one else's dream of having it all, of growth at any cost?

I am creating my business in a way that is balanced between the time to connect deeply with my own creative and soulful pursuits, whether that be through play, story telling, dance, art, mosaic or horses. I have time for stillness and for being in nature. I create time to cook wholesome meals and enjoy the garden. All of these pursuits are sources of inspiration for the wisdom I share with my clients.

My family holds a high priority. I work wherever I am, whether that be from a temporary office on the beach in Cambodia, whilst visiting one son or whilst volunteering with my other son in his NGO www.onegirl.org.au in Sierra Leone.
I take time out to connect and enjoy both my brother and sister's company on holidays whilst still writing and coaching in a way that flows with ease and grace.
I am able to swim or walk in the morning, have stimulating conversations about global issues with a German tourist who I may meet on my walk and then return home to writing or coaching. During the day I may be interviewed by a magazine over Skype, or have a mentoring call. I plan my time to write to share what is valuable for my clients and I am more productive than I have ever been. Life is good. Business is good.

There is much work to be done but all in it's own time whilst valuing what is important in the whole of my life, moment by moment. This is the possibility for a successful life as a professional Thought Leader.

Success in whole of life terms is also possible in some organisations today. With organisations such as GOOGLE leading the way, work is more like a community where balancing, health, relationships and fulfilment in a contribution to business purpose, all contribute to success. It is my wish that more organisations embrace what it is to be successful in whole of life terms as the boundaries between of work and life become blurred, let us not forego our personal needs.

To conclude.

To be successful by choice, in your terms, consider these questions:

- What is it that you most value?
- What is the intention of your life?
- For yourself?
- For your family?

- For your work?
- Are your actions valuing the things that you say you value?
- What is falling through the cracks?
- Will having more and growing a business or competing at work give you your heart desires or not?
- How much is enough?
- What information are you not listening to from your sensory body and emotions?
- What happens when you do not trust yourself, your "gut" instincts about making your choices?
- All of our answers will be different for these questions. We all have different, circumstances and different needs.

Remember what you value and hold it dearly.

You may want to change some things in your life and your work, but not all things need changing, not all things need growing.

Some just require care, maintenance, love and tenderness.

Deborah Lange is an Award Winning Mentor, writer, speaker, coach for accessing a new suite of sensory and intuitive capacities to embrace wholeness in our life and create the success we desire in our own terms. Her new book which goes into more detail of the, "Intuit Your Truth for Success", model will be published late in 2015. You can contact her at www.deblange.com deborahlange@mac.com

This is a significant context for this chapter. The work I undertook to understand what I was doing, thinking and feeling from both the past and the present has been valuable in re-claiming my success today. My work has also significantly contribute to young Gen X, Gen Y and Millennial's who sought me out to when they had the foresight to want to stand on some-one else's shoulders who had been there before them and learn the skills I learnt earlier in life.

"Something I am doing is working and I am successful at work. But something I am doing is not and I want to understand why and transform what I am doing that is sabotaging my success."

Deborah Lange

About the author

Deborah Lange is an Award Winning Mentor, writer, speaker, coach for accessing a new suite of sensory and intuitive capacities to embrace wholeness in our life and create the success we desire in our own terms. Her new book which goes into more detail of the "Intuit Your Truth for Success", model will be published late in 2015. You can contact her at
www.deblange.com
deborahlange@mac.com

HOW TO START A BUSINESS WITH LITTLE OR NO CASH

EDITED BY KIZZI NKWOCHA

How Do You Measure Your Success?

So you have just worked very hard and bought your new car. Are you a success now?
When the car is two years old and the novelty has worn out, are you still a success?
This is an interesting point to ponder. How do we measure our success? Is it by the car we drive, the money we have in the bank, the choices that we make, the freedom we have or the quality times we have with family and friends?
The dictionary defines success as having achieved our goals or having obtained wealth, status, achievements and honour.
Every one of us is an individual and we would all have our true definition and meaning as to what success is. We can be successful in some aspects of our lives and not successful in others. We can be successful in love, in our career, in money, in parenting or in all aspects of our life. Wouldn't it be good to just feel successful and let that be enough? There is no need for any more, as enough is enough.
So let's talk about money. We all need money, money is like air, and we cannot live without it. We all have bills to pay, food and clothes to buy and we all like to be entertained. Even when you live off the grid and are self sufficient you still have to have money. Somehow the land you live on will be rented or purchased in the majority of cases. Certainly when we have more money in the bank this allows us to have more freedom of choices that we can make. The bottom line is that money does not make us who we are, it is our beliefs and our behaviours that make us who we are and we are able to change these at will, if we have the desire and motivation to do so.
We have choices in life and a choice we have is to ask ourselves "Do we want to live in the Dead Zone or the Alive Zone?"
There are many of us who choose to be part of the walking dead zone, working at a job we are good at or a job we have to do to pay our bills. So often we get directed to things in life that we academically are good at, our parents want us to do or our career advisor advised us to do. We follow the sheep and do what is expected of us and so we play the game of happy families. The truth of the matter is that a lot of families are just living and existing and they are not bursting at the seams with life.

There are many living out there, chasing the dollar and working hard to get to a certain place, believing that when they reach this certain place the empty feeling inside will subside. When we live like this we are always living for the future and the sad thing about that is that we forget the here and now. Life can pass us by very quickly, children grow up and precious moments can get lost. If you are waiting for enlightenment and to live happily ever after, then keep waiting. Nirvana rarely comes as life continues to bring us more lessons to learn, gifts to bestow and choices. There is always more and it ever ends. Life does reward action, to create success in your life, you need to take action. Action with feeling works even better. Wouldn't it be nice to be successful in the life you are living now and to create a wealth of precious memories and times?

There are people out there who have financial stability and yet still feel somehow unfulfilled and unsatisfied inside. Then there are people who are happy and content living meagre lives and having simple needs. We are all different....Thankfully. Having lots of money in the bank will never replace emptiness that we feel inside, though it might make living easier. A successful like is one where we find our inner happiness.

Would you like to wake up every morning saying 'Yipee, another glorious day,' as we spend our day doing what we are passionate about or that we dream about? Life can leave us feeling trapped or it can leave us feeling excited. We can also become trapped in the trappings and material items we buy. It is time to let go of the need for recognition, to look good to others, of the image of being a nice affluent person and to get real. This is the essence of success.

How many of us are happy in our own skin? How many of us are successful at really and I mean really loving yourself and seeing yourself for all the wonderful, positive and divine things that you do and are. We forget that we are so much more than these bodies and thoughts. We are divine beings with ultimate intelligence, wisdom and eternal energy. Once we are able to connect to this inner or higher aspect of ourselves, then we find that we are never truly alone. There is always more and we can connect to ourselves in a more successful and meaningful way. That is success and it can easily be achieved through meditation, body movement, taking responsibility for you and letting go of any baggage that weighs you down.

So what about shoulds vs musts? We all have gifts and talents in different aspects of our lives, like I have said before, we are all individuals. Is the thing you are doing now a must or a should? A should is something that others believe we are best doing, it has an element of control attached to it. It is the thing that others desire us to be and do and it is for their benefit not ours. A must is something that is like an inner voice inside us saying 'I must do this ...., doing this makes me feel alive.'

Life is meant for living. Life is for us to feel present in our bodies, to feel connected to our beliefs, desires, feelings, loves and losses. There is a certain sense of succeeding when we feel at home in our bodies and we come home to ourselves. It is better to feel the love from another and the hurt of pain, rather than to feel nothing at all. Start to take some chances, get out of the auto pilot seat and get into the driving seat of your life. Start doing the hobbies and creative things that you have always wanted to do now.

Success is about the value we place on ourselves, the beauty that we see in life, the quality time we have with those we love, the acknowledgement of a beautiful sunrise or the fun we have with friends and family. It is the feeling that these things give us, that measures how successful we are. What is your value? How much are you worth for your time per hour? Do you feel comfortable doubling this hourly rate?

For us to be successful we have to be free first and foremost. Having freedom gives us more choices in life. When you feel free what will your life look like, what will you see yourself doing and what will you hear others saying to you? Where in your body will you feel this feeling most? Will it have a colour, shape, texture or temperature? Ask yourself why do you want to be free? What are the things that you would do and why?

Once we start to think in this way the laws of attraction start to step in and we start to bring more beautiful and abundant things into our life. If you are in a 'bad' space then it is time to 'Fake it until you make it.' Hold your head up high, stand tall and look to start taking yourself to a better place. This is the path to success.

Every single thought we have puts out a message to the universe. The universe always provides and will willingly provide us with all we want and desire. That part is easy. The part of this process that can stop the world of success coming closer to us our very own resistance to having it. Where there is resistance this is an indication that maybe this is not the right path for us. Follow the path of least resistance. Follow the feel good feeling. Hang around with people who are positive, supportive, fun and make you feel good.

For the success we desire to come to us, we have to line up to the vibration of success and abundance. We have to live it, breathe it, act it and be it. We have to walk the talk and be the reality that we want to create. We have to make our businesses work for us and not us work for our businesses. We have to have fun, laugh, enjoy the success of the company we keep, the friends we have and the things that we do.

Friends are very important. Who are the closest five people in your life? How positive are they? What habits and behaviours do they have? What income do they make? It is said that the closest people to us are a reflection of who we are. As we choose to change and grow, we find at times, the friends we used to hang around, just do not seem to stimulate us or make us feel happy anymore. This is inner growth and us valuing who we are and how we choose to spend our time as our time is precious. It is time to let go freely and move onto the next ladder of life.

It is worth looking at the underlying beliefs we have about being succeeding and those being successful. People can often create an opinion or easily judge according to the beliefs they have been raised with. How do you feel about successful people? Do you relish in their good fortune, or do you think they must have done something dishonest to get to where they are? Explore your beliefs because if you cannot celebrate other's good fortune, then you will be resisting yours. Those who have come from rags to riches will have done so with setbacks in their lives, hard work, dedication and a passion to succeed. Do you have this in you? `

The ironic thing is once you start feeling better about who and what you are, the priorities in your life will start to change. You may no longer want to chance the dollar; instead you look for quality time. You no longer are working hard you start to work wise. You no longer want to be a millionaire, you what to have an enjoyable and happy lifestyle. You no longer want to be a taker, you start to become a giver and this is what humanity needs right now.

It is of great importance that we feel good about ourselves. How can others feel important about us, if we don't feel important about ourselves? Get your values aligned and go to that good feeling place. When you put yourself first it does not mean you are selfish, it means that you are self loving. You are connecting to yourself, acknowledging your needs and desires and then doing what you want to do to have these needs met.

Motivation.....What is your motivation?

We all have things in life that drive us forward, it can be the desire for money, for fame, for recognition, for status, for success, for creativity, for helping humanity or for satisfaction. Once you know what motivates you, you can use it as leverage to get the energy flowing and to get the motivation happening. You will have a greater understanding of what fulfils you. You will have an end goal and the setting of goals is very important. People who set themselves goals achieve far more than those that do not.

In your career and business world, start to look for points of leverage. Quality connections are worth spending time following up. We can spend time connecting to 100 people, though of that 100 people there might only be 2 or 3 that provide us with what we want. It may be time to reduce the dead zone or dead end connections and to start following the leverage leads. Quality leads and quality time with people that you like is important to keep us in that feel good space. What would you rather have in your life, quality or quantity?

Learn to take small steps forward. When setting goals think about where you would like to be in 10 years time? Now ask yourself where would you like to be in 5 years time? What will you be doing, how will you look and what does it feel like? The next step will be to ask yourself what you will have to do to achieve this. From this point you can start some goal setting. Long-term and short term goals work well. When you have explored the things in life that fulfil you, you can create your long term goals around this. Aim to make your goals measureable, so then you will be able to monitor your progress and once you find you are stepping off track you will have to make functional changes to help get you back on track.

Taking small steps to start with will show benefits down the track. That extra phone call you make everyday ads up to 730 extra phone calls after two years. That extra 10 minutes of exercise ads up to 7,300 minutes after two years. That one less chocolate bar every day, adds up to 645,320 calories after two years. These small steps have a large impact overtime. What is needed for this to happen is persistence and discipline. Make these small steps enjoyable and achievable. After a while you might even get to like them. It is important for you to do what makes you happy, because life is supposed to be fun.

Remember that small opportunities can lead into larger opportunities.

In what order would you place spirituality, family, relationships, career and money? And how can you integrate the success in all of these? It is possible to connect these different aspects of your life and to have a good balance between them all. The word enthusiasm means "God Within." This does not mean there is a man sitting up there in his chair, looking down on you and passing judgment. Enthusiasm is that connected feeling that you have that encompasses words like spirituality, energy, vivacity, eagerness and passion. Wouldn't it be great to have more of this in your life?

When we have a sense of spirituality it allows our intuition to grow. Our intuition is a wonderful guidance system and one very often not used enough. The more we work this muscle and trust this muscle the more it will go. You will get a sense of ringing a certain person at a certain time, going to a certain seminar or workshop at a certain date. This is the intuition working for you. When you have the goal of being and feeling a success, then you will be guided to where you need to be. You do have to learn to listen, the intuition can be quite subtle in the beginning and it can easily be forgotten. Once again deepening the connection with yourself will work the intuition muscle.

Once we deepen our inner connection, this increases the depth of the connection that we have with others in our lives. We can become kinder at heart, compassionate, forgiving, giving and empathetic. There are times when we can give the simplest of time and energy to those around us and it can have larger implications in providing trust, loyalty and friendship. It pays to give a little, though not of you. Remember a 'free you' first.

When we are connected and grounded in who and what we are then we react less and act more. We do not become upset what others think or say about us, instead it is far more important what we think of believe about them.

In summary, success is what you want it to mean to you. It does compass a sense of achievement and feeling good and as I have said before, life is supposed to be fun. Fun stands for feeling Free, Uninhibited and Natural. This is enough.

Louise Plant

About the author

Louise Plant is an Entrepreneur, Holistic Nutritionist, Master Herbalist, Life Transformer, Mover and Shaker.
She is a motivated, passionate and illuminated speaker, author, facilitator, teacher and healer.
She has been teaching for over 25 years in all aspects of Herbal Medicine, Holistic Living, Nutrition, Spiritual Growth and Emotional Healing.
Her qualifications include Diplomas in Naturopathy, Remedial Therapies, Animal Homeopathy, Honours Diploma is Herbal Medicine,
Certificate in Business Management, Bachelors Degree in Natural Science and a Post Grad in Higher Education.
Her passions are travel, adventure, functional foods, healing plants, learning new concepts, empowering others, bringing families together, healing humanity and laughing with my family.
She loves to see the light being turned on inside people, and seeing them 'light up' as they reconnect to their bodies and themselves.

Her latest venture is Vitae Amor Seminars which is a series of Seminars that create a safe and nurturing environment for participants to access and release emotional and mental baggage.

www.louiseplant.com.au   www.vitaeamorseminars.com.au

Wellbeing through harmony

One of the main threats to our wellbeing is stress. Stress can cause psychological disorders which become physical illness - digestive disorders, cardiac disease and cancers. Many do not consider the stress in our lives caused by unresolved conflict.
Hold a glass of water in your outstretched hand. It's easy to do. Hold it there for a few moments. That's ok too. Try holding it for a few hours and your arm will be really sore. The longer you hold it, the more difficult it becomes. We understand that the weight of the glass has not changed. It's our capacity to keep it holding it up. It's the same with stress caused by unresolved conflict.
It is natural to feel discomfort when dealing with conflict. We fear the consequences of that conversation. How will we feel? How would the conversation go? What could the outcomes be? Could there be more harm caused than good? What will the reaction of the other person be? What if they are so hurt or upset with us that our relationship is damaged? We fear the consequences of such an uncomfortable conversation.
I had a conversation with a woman whose relationship with her brother was damaged because of a misunderstanding about what she had said decades ago. When I asked if she had ever attempted to speak about it with him, she looked astonished at the question and then said "No. That would only make things worse." Their relationship was more cautious and cooler because of long held incorrect beliefs and suspicion.
The easiest direction is downhill, but it is a dangerous one, and that is the way most relationships head when conflict is not managed well. Our genetics teach us to flight, fight or freeze, and none of these are very useful to us any longer. The flight fight, freeze response comes from the ancient part of our brains called the amygdala, and its original purpose was a lifesaving one. Should we have been confronted by a dangerous animal, we would get a rush of adrenalin and blood to fuel our muscles to help us to run away faster if we could, fight if we had to defend ourselves or freeze in case the creature hadn't noticed us or would be more entertained by chasing one of our friends who had chosen the flight or fight response.

With blood loaded in our muscles we have starved the resourceful (modern, thinking) part of our brain which enables our rational mind (in the frontal cortex) to work. It is not possible to think as creatively and clearly when in flight, fight or freeze. There aren't too many wild animals to contend with in our modern era, so the flight, fight, freeze response is no longer required as much as it was for our ancient forebears.

In conflict, to flight is to avoid. Conflict does make us feel uncomfortable and we often choose the avoidance path as the easy downhill option. We may avoid a conversation via the fight response, by arguing, trying to overpower, convince, coerce, using raised voices or threatening tones, it may even denigrate to physical violence. We may avoid a conversation using the freeze response, just pretending it didn't happen, getting "over it" and living with the accumulation of feelings of disappointment, and then resentment.

None of these ways of responding to conflict ever really resolves the issues. There is a fourth response that most people have not learned, and that is to think, to listen and consider what the other person is really saying, build understanding, to discuss and if needed, find new options that are mutually acceptable. The problem with this conversation avoided, is that the conflict has gone unresolved. A small conflict may blow over the first time, and may be even next, however soon we are likely to be feeling highly stressed. The longer this conflict goes on, the more uncomfortable (think of the glass of water) we feel. At some stage, when a situation arises with that person, or someone else if we are now very highly stressed, we are likely to explode. The person who is at the other end of our outburst will be wondering what ever is wrong with us. What a bad tempered and unpleasant person we are and certainly undesirable to be around. An observer may judge us our bad behaviour negatively and avoid getting to know us as a person.

Each person has their own truth and perception is their reality. Consider two next-door neighbours who live in houses divided by a shoulder height fence. They have been chatting across the fence about their gardens and then one mentions that they don't like the colour of their blue fence. The other says they quite like it and it is not really blue it is more of a green colour. The first insists that it is nothing like green, and calls their family out to comment on the colour. Each says that yes, it is definitely blue. The other neighbour also calls out their family to back them up. That family says, no way is it blue it can only be called green. The families have taken sides and help to strengthen the position and resolve of the neighbour with the dispute. At the same time they may be denigrating the other neighbour to each other and to their friends. Each friend has their own war story to add to the conversation and the conflict escalates.

As mediators we hear stories once they get to the stage of hurt, upset and pain. As much as we care, we cannot believe any one person's story. If we did, we would be expecting the other party to be a bad person! What I do believe is that it is *their* truth. When I speak with other party (or parties) naturally their version is always very different from the first person's story. Some say there are always two sides to every story. I say there are always at least three, each person's side and what really happened – and then there is their history to consider.

As mediators we can help each party go to take a look at the other person's side of their fence and see that perhaps it is actually painted a different colour on each side and that both are equally correct and incorrect, it just depends on their point of view.

It reminds me of a joke – An elderly man goes to the doctor because his wife is going deaf and she won't admit it. She refuses to go to the doctor because she says her hearing is fine. He asked the doctor how he could work out how deaf she actually was. The doctor suggested when he got home, he should go into the furthest room of the house and speak in a normal voice. Then move to the next closest and then the next, speaking at a normal voice each time and take note of when she hears him. So he did that.

Whilst his wife was in the kitchen he went to the furthest part of the house and asked "What's for dinner dear?" There was no answer, so he moved into the next room and asked again "What's for dinner dear?" There was still no answer, so he moved into the next room and asked again "What's for dinner dear?" When there was no answer at that short distance he began feeling very concerned for her. He went up right behind her and asked in a normal speaking voice "What's for dinner dear?" to which she replied, "For goodness sakes Frank, I've told you three times, CHICKEN!"

In my experience, everybody in dispute thinks they are right, otherwise they would not be in dispute. Each holds a position and the more firmly they hold their position the less capable of being able to listen to others and certainly not consider their point of view. They resolutely believe in the strength of their conviction because they have lived history of the conflict, seen, felt and heard "their truth." This can get to a level where one or both (or all) become high conflict personalities (HCPs). The HCP has a mistaken perception of danger, and they resort to the fight response. The HCP will blame, and accuse. Everything is the other person's fault, never theirs. Arguing with this person is futile, it only reinforces their belief that we are unreasonable and argumentative. They don't understand why we don't agree with them and will continue to defend their position, gaining strength from their victories when their fight overwhelms others and causes them to retreat. When both or all parties are at this level, violence can erupt and it is likely they will part company. The stronger their conviction the more they own their position. For an HCP to admit they are wrong, would bruise their fragile ego, and they would lose face, and they would never allow that. There are ways of dealing with HCPs and professional mediators may the best way to help you work with them.

It can be dangerous to try to reason with the unreasonable, whether they be HCP, affected by drugs or alcohol. Remember safety is paramount.

Sometimes people who have sustained long term conflict, feel trapped in a relationship and they become withdrawn, expecting and waiting for the next outburst. This is an abusive, bullying relationship and the cycle of abuse is well documented. It happens between people who regularly spend time together in families, in workplaces and in social situations. It is worse when there is a physical, emotional or hierarchical power imbalance.

Typically the cycle of abuse starts with an escalating conflict. The escalation can be slow or it can happen more quickly if the cycle has been repeated often in the past. The escalation results in an outburst of anger, denigration and abuse, sometimes violence, harming the "victim." The one who abused the other may recognise that their abuse has caused the other person to react – crying, withdrawing, sometimes even apologising for making the abuser angry. The abuser, fearing loss of the relationship and as a result (they may feel genuinely sorry and ashamed at the time), their power, apologises, makes promises not to behave so badly again and then there is a honeymoon stage, where things are pleasant. During the honeymoon, the abuser may bestow gifts and favours upon their victim.

Unfortunately the honeymoon can only be sustained for a short while. The nature of this type of relationship means that it won't be very long before stress builds again, the abuser, driven by their own fears, distress and feelings of danger, perceives an action or a word of their victim, who has been walking on eggshells, as an affront against them, and they become angry again. The cycle repeats. Usually, the longer the cycle repeats the shorter the honeymoon period until it disappears and all that is left is stress, from crisis after crisis, abuse after abuse. The long term result is a victim feeling helpless and hopeless, believing that they are part of this problem, and that they are trapped. They often believe that the abuser really loves them and needs them, and that if they did get out, they'd have no happy alternatives, and that their reality, really is not so bad. They believe that they just need to find ways of not making them angry. This cycle can be learned and repeated by generations and over the years in workplaces where it is believed and expect it as normal.

The loss of self-esteem caused by protracted abuse means that victims have lost confidence in their own ability to cope. Often when victims do escape such an abusive relationship or workplace, they are drawn to another because that is what they are used to and may feel they deserve. These victims need to find help. There are domestic violence advice centres in most cities and regional areas in Australia. Workplaces and clubs are protected by Fair Work Australia, and various ombudsmen.

Perpetrators of bullying, abuse and violence also need to seek help to curb their "uncontrollable" outbursts of anger and abuse. The cycle needs to be stopped.

In workplaces anti-bullying legislation is in place. Workplaces have policies and codes of conduct which address bullying when utilised correctly. All workers in the workplace, from the most senior to the most junior are responsible for workplace safety and this includes bullying. Workplace bullying needs to be identified, prevented and managed effectively and it is vital that all workers are trained to know what to do if it happens to them or if they witness others being bullied. It is just as important that those whose behaviours are identified as being bullying, recognise and stop or they will be forced to leave. Specialised independent anti-bullying training for workplaces can be found on the link www.bullyresponse.com.au

Unfortunately families don't have written codes of conduct or policies, and behind closed doors domestic violence is an appalling problem that only family values and public campaigns can address. Because of the systemic nature of family violence, extended family may not be helpful, friends are often ignorant of the situation and it is often up to the victim to leave and seek help, if they are able to. Children learn that abuse is "normal" and they model their own relationships on their parents', often repeating the abuse cycle with their own relationships, and so it goes.

In many families there is a definite hierarchy, this is often cultural. Much of the time it is the male (sometimes female) who has the final say. It may be the eldest sibling who has been made responsible for their younger siblings. As long as the system works for the family there can be harmony and productivity. Unfortunately this often leads to the "leader" feeling privileged and entitled. They may use inappropriate behaviour to assert their power. Shouting, swearing, belittling, intimidating, ignoring other's needs, threatening, posturing and physical violence add up to domestic violence. Domestic abuse may be verbal, physical, emotional, psychological, financial, religious, sexual, even cyber. There is no point in blaming anyone when abuse is systemic. It just has to stop!

Interestingly, not every person who comes from an abusive home repeats the cycle. Many recognise domestic violence and abuse as a problem and never repeat it.

Education about healthy ways to resolve conflict is vital, but sadly lacking. When we understand that the purpose of conflict is to recognise it as a reason to talk, to work things out and improve a situation for the benefit of all, then we have no need to fear it. We can actually embrace conflict as a catalyst for positive change. Instead conflict of escalating it can be managed – most of the time.

There will always be HCPs to deal with occasionally, however rather than being a victim of their aggressive and defensive behaviour through our natural flight, fight or freeze responses, we can do something else instead. Bill Eddy in his book It's All Your Fault says that we can use Empathy, Attention, Respect and Set Limits, they would be very unlikely to find themselves in that situation. Nobody would need to be an abuser, and others would have healthy boundaries to help protect them from being victimised.

Trying to manage conflict effectively with an HCP, may be only possible with professional assistance such as mediation. Go to www.interMEDIATE.com.au for more information.

So is abuse always learned or can it be personality? Many parents will tell you that one of their children was naturally aggressive whilst the others were passive. Children who are aggressive need to be taught effective ways to resolve their problems without resorting to aggression.

Not long ago, I witnessed a woman yelling very aggressively to her son who appeared to be about eight years old. The son reacted to her in exactly the same tone and aggressive body language. I wondered how the others in their household treated each other and imagined that he may grow into a very aggressive adult who will treat his "loved ones" the same way.

Many people believe that people cannot change. We believe they can, with proper education from experts, or through being compelled. The first way means gaining understanding of the problem and what needs to be done and how to do it. The second way, to be compelled, may be made through laws. Some years ago people used to smoke in hospitals, planes, busses, restaurants, schools and indeed anywhere they wanted to. I remember my doctor smoking in his rooms during a consultation. With an overflowing ashtray on his desk he probably told people with lung complaints, that they should quit smoking. Another example is seatbelts. As a child we had no seatbelts, we would just jump into the back seat of the car away we'd go. Laws have changed and so have our attitudes.

Sometimes an event causes realisation which ensures we change. There is an old story I love to tell: An admiral was at the helm of his ship one night. The brass buttons on his smart uniform reflecting the lights on the bridge of the ship. In the distance he can see a small light and realises that his ship is heading towards it. A voice comes across his radio "You are on a collision course with us and we suggest you change direction by 3degrees north." The admiral, knowing his important standing replied gruffly with an air or superiority "This is the admiral of Her Majesty's Steam Ship Orion, you change course" and the voice from the light in the distance said "This is Private JJ Smith, and this is a lighthouse." The captain changed his course. Just realising the consequences of our actions can change our attitude and our actions.

The best time to discuss a conflict is early, before it has had a chance to escalate.

Importantly, safety must come first.

It is helpful to invite the person you need to have a half hour conversation with you. Suggest some times that would suit you and invite them to choose one that works for them as well. You can do this face to face, by phone or in writing. Let them know that you would really like to sort things out amicably. If you are doing it in writing you may propose an agenda and ask them if they have anything they would like to add. You may even give them a copy of this book so they understand what you now do, about conflict.

Ensure the relationship is more important than the conflict. This conversation is not to be viewed as your opportunity to blame, to tell the other what they did wrong or to berate anyone. They won't hear what you are saying, and it will likely damage the relationship further.

Communication is 56% tone, 35% - 37% body language and just 8% the words you choose, so be aware of the true message that comes across.

Set the scene. Meeting in a neutral place like a coffee shop where there is the opportunity to feel more relaxed than in your home, your office or theirs. It's also more private, away from the eyes and ears of the curious.

Order refreshments and enjoy them for a few moments if you can.

Thank the other person for agreeing to talk with you and check they have put aside the half hour.

After breaking the ice with some questions that show you care, such as how they are, their family, their work etc. state the problem that you need to address. Let them know that you understand they may see things differently and invite their input. Ask if they have any questions about what you said.

At all times remain respectful.

Let them talk about how they see the problem. Remember you have two ears and one mouth and they need to be used in that ratio. Listen.

Some people think that listening is waiting for the other person to say a few words and then saying what they want to say without even really taking on board what has been said by the other person. To really listen, ask questions about what the other person has said to you.

Separate the person from the problem. You are both dealing with the same problem, even though you see it very differently, so try not to think that it is the person who IS the problem.

Don't bring up old issues that have nothing to do with the issue you are dealing with. Doing so will only divert the conversation to other areas and the issue you are meant to be speaking about will not be resolved.

A little bit of empathy goes a long way. If they state that have been suffering because of your dispute, empathise e.g. "It sounds like it has been really tough for you." Try to understand from their point of view and then state your concerns.

Stay calm.

If things heat up, take a break.

Time out is a great strategy at times when we are feeling distressed, angry, upset, or otherwise emotionally incapable of speaking with clarity and respect. There are three parts to a time out, first is the communication that you need it, say how long you require. It may be as soon as 10 minutes if you are only mildly upset, or 48 hours if you feel very angry. Then the person who calls time out, must resume that conversation at the end of the agreed time. If people are still feeling incapable, perhaps another time out may be required.

Never attempt to resolve conflict when the other person is really angry. If anger is directed at you ask for time out. Time out gives you and the other person some time to cool down.

Once the half hour is up, thank the person once again for working together with you.

Arrange another time to catch up if you feel confident, to review what you have agreed to.

People who cannot manage their own conflict, usually believe that mediation is a great thing, but it won't work for them. Somehow their situation is different to others, too difficult and too large, the other person too obstinate. We agree that every situation *is* unique, however most people who make a genuine attempt at mediation will find it does work for them. Nationally Accredited Mediators are skilled and trained to work with people in conflict.

Mediation has an extremely high success rate and can be used for families, workplaces, clubs, communities, schools, even between countries in conflict. Mediation helps to restore important relationships, it helps keep people out of expensive, stressful and protracted court processes.

We did a workplace mediation for two female colleagues who had a highly emotional about their issues. It was a long standing conflict but it had been largely ignored because they worked in two physically distant areas of one building. One was being promoted to a job in the other one's office. Although she wanted the new job, neither could stand the thought of working together.

Their CEO called us and we provided each with Initial Assessments to enable us to have a thorough insight into their situation before deciding whether it was suitable for mediation. Both were highly emotional and did not want to work together in mediation. They had been "voluntold." When asked, neither could name any other way of resolving the issue, and they agreed to give mediation a try.

We ensured they both had Non-Participating Support Persons and they did manage to work together, being guided by us throughout the five hour process. We helped them to identify the causes of their issues, to discuss them and find some new options to resolve their dispute. There were acknowledgments and apologies. Once they had negotiated their own agreement, they were so relieved they both cried again, and hugged each other. We phoned some time later to see if they were able to work productively and in harmony, and the CEO asked "What did you do, they've been on happy pills!"

In our case, we utilise a very powerful co-model of mediation. Co-mediation utilises the strengths and skills of two mediators working together as a team. A female and male mediator is gender balanced, so it is very unlikely any party will feel the mediation is biased against them. Because of this, most people feel it is a fairer process. It is also more effective and efficient and allows documents to be crafted and printed in session. This increases the chances of a robust agreement that all parties can live with.

We also include an education component to our mediation which helps people to identify how their conflict style helps or hinders communication, and teach them some new skills for resolving their conflicts in a respectful and effective way in the future.

With the dispute resolved and harmony restored people can get on with their lives without the burden holding them back from true happiness and wellbeing.

Naomi Holtring

About the author

Naomi holds a Master's Degree in Dispute Resolution from the Law Faculty of UTS. Co-Director, she is Managing Partner of interMEDIATE, a Nationally Accredited Mediator, workplace trainer, facilitator. NLP Practitioner, member of LEADR, and Current Board member of ADRA (Australian Dispute Resolution Association). Naomi has chaired and presented at the inaugural Bullying Conference in Sydney billing the Fair Work Commission. She has been a conference convenor with the NSW Department of Juvenile Justice since 2010 and is listed on the NSW Police panel for mediation. Naomi has mediated and trained staff in government departments and delivered training in identification, prevention and management of bullying and harassment in the workplace for numerous schools, hospitals and community-based organisation.

She is specialised in areas including, but not limited to, workplace dispute resolution, Co-mediation, mediation, facilitation, supervision and conflict management coaching., facilitation, supervision and conflict management coaching.

The Three Pillars Of Success

Most people fear failure. We tend not to seize opportunities for success - no matter what our definition of success might be. We lay blame to an underlying fear of rejection or criticism, finding excuses for not taking action and moving forward.

Instead we remain stuck, oblivious to the immense potential we possess and are capable of summoning. We fumble around having no concept of the true value we have to offer the world, nor the skills or talents we wield, let alone allow ourselves to find a passion or purpose in life. Here's why: It all boils down to programming and a set of beliefs we have about our capabilities.

Successful people believe they are more than capable of achieving success. They don't feel they are lacking in any way, they find solutions to any hurdles, weaknesses or distractions, aiming for a life that's far from mediocre. It doesn't matter how they started out, they have an inner belief that they are only a few steps away from having that perfect holiday, or owning that mansion or Ferrari, because they know their own worth.

They don't wait for opportunities, they create them. They believe in their destiny and align their actions accordingly.

Why then, do the rest of us manage our lives like fire stations? We inertly wait for something bad to happen and take reactive measures. We wait to hit rock-bottom, or for our stress levels to escalate before we take the time to alter our approach. Because change can be challenging.

When we are already overwhelmed or drowning in our circumstances, we have no clue where to start, or how, another challenge to our added routine can feel rather burdensome or quite daunting. Going down a new path that we are entirely unfamiliar with comes across as risky and unappealing.

But what if we were to know the end outcome? What if we were to believe that we would reach our destination, no matter what challenge came up ahead? Or that each challenge would in fact, help us grow and learn in order to become wholly successful and thoroughly experienced in life?

Taking on a new journey takes commitment, practice, and authenticity – words that can be scary and make us feel vulnerable. The challenge of eating healthy and exercising regularly, for example, can come across monotonous or frightening to many of us. However, with utmost dedication, engaging in positive habits and regular reflection on our progress and performing revisions, we can attain lasting feelings of self-satisfaction and self-worth.

Pillar One – Build a Compelling Vision

According to Sir Isaac Newton's First Law of Motion, objects in motion tend to stay in motion, and objects at rest tend to stay at rest unless acted upon by an unbalanced force.

Many of us remain idle, not only because we lack a driving force, but we tend to sabotage our creativity or inspiration which ordinarily keeps us motivated. Finding clarity and steering the ship in the right direction can be made less intimidating when people have a compelling vision.

Creative visualisation uses imagination to make dreams and goals come true. It can vastly improve one's life and attract success and prosperity. Visualisations can stimulate the sympathetic nervous system, which governs our fight-or-flight response and cause increased heart rate, breathing, and blood pressure. Through mental images, one can literally confuse the body into believing the mental scene or image is actually happening to them. The visualisation creates a conflict in the subconscious mind that focuses solely on explaining the difference between where they currently are, to where they see themselves to be, and calculates the possibilities to achieve those outcomes. This is a powerful way of bringing you into contact with new people, situations and circumstances. The subconscious mind changes our mindset accordingly, and aligns our habits and actions.

Research has shown that surgeons, musicians, athletes and entrepreneurs can successfully use mental imagery to improve their motivation and performance. It could help them run a marathon, excel at a presentation, or pass up an enticing dessert.

So how do people use the power of visualization to bring their dreams to fruition? Below are the main steps for making it work in your life.

1. Close your eyes and sit in a quiet place without distractions
2. Breathe deeply and exhale slowly
3. Repeat three times as you relax all the muscles in your body
4. Visualise an event or scene describing what you truly desire in your life
5. Freeze the image and use all the five senses to absorb the entire scene, including the still objects, the surroundings and your own emotions
6. Take as long as you need to mentally record everything
7. Breathe out and release the image, and open your eyes

Write down the details and create affirmations that hold true to your visualisation. Each morning as you wake, visualize this scene and take at least one action towards making it a reality. Whenever you can, take action and keep an open mind for any ideas, insight and possibilities.

Many people also create Vision Boards, therefore creating a physical representation of the mental image that they can view any time to remind them of their goals and outcomes. This is a powerful technique to bring abundance and prosperity into all areas of your life.

Pillar Two – Build a Resource Pack

Connecting with like-minded people and building a networking community is easier than some might think given all of the social tools and applications available today. Reaching out to someone in the local community, sending an email to a friend or colleague to ask a question or for support, creating a Facebook page, or even a small support group are just some examples of available resources. In reality, there are endless possibilities waiting to be explored.

All successful people have a supportive group of people cheering them on their visions. It is vital to their success and minimizes the chances of self-sabotage or feelings of isolation and confusion. Mentors, colleagues, coaches, and the local community are often happy to serve as a resource. And sometimes, they too get inspired along the way.

If you find yourself wondering about available resources, you need only ask. The subconscious mind will find a way to bring them into reality. Keep in mind the resources that you already have on the journey with you: the support of family and friends, your own motivation and determination, years of experience, thinking and learning, your skills and talents, your character, strengths, and of course, your vision. These are all resources and strengths to draw from, as you navigate your path to success through life.

The important thing is to think creatively about your needs, and exhaust all the available options to find resources that meet those needs.

Each resource should be aimed to help you navigate your vision and encourage reflection, assist in preparation and planning, promote the use of other resources, and answer concerns or questions as you progress towards your success.

Be proactive. Establish relationships, gain more knowledge and share your ideas and concerns. By doing so, you can maintain a strong support network that will keep you on track as you progress through your ultimate vision for success.

Pillar Three – Build Your Mindset

As most people embark on this mammoth journey, a voice inside begins to bring up numerous concerns like "Do you really think it's possible? Maybe you're not good enough" or, "What if you fail? You will forever be seen as a failure." "People will laugh at you for having such ridiculous ideas." "Maybe if I just avoid it, it will go away and I can be safe from putting myself out there. I will be able to protect my dignity and save myself the heartache."

It's time to decide how important the vision really is to them and whether it's worth the risk.

Is it better to remain safe, or live the life I want? I may eventually get there, but it will be difficult – is that a choice I'm willing to make right now?

Let's say they choose to move forward. As they hit a hurdle, the voice appears again, "You knew this wouldn't work out, maybe you can drop it while it's still early." "See, now you've gone and shown the world how ridiculous you are." "They were all right. It's not too late to back out, make excuses, and try to regain your dignity."

Each new step on the journey to success brings new challenges. Yet, there is always a choice. Continue or quit.

It's amazing how most of us will procrastinate on things that aren't actually difficult to do, we all have the talent and skills to accomplish them, yet we avoid pursuing them for one reason or another. Our insecurities seem to get the better of us. Self-sabotage creeps in and keeps us 'safe' and playing small. Successful people have a different mindset, they are determined to get to their destination, regardless of setbacks. They will find the resources (internal or external) to overcome their adversities and meet their expectations.

Carol Dweck, psychologist and author of the book 'Mindset', believes that one of the most basic beliefs we carry about ourselves has to do with simple qualities, like intelligence or talent. She outlines that those who have a "fixed mindset" believe that their character, intelligence, and creativity are fixed traits that cannot be changed easily, and success comes inherently without much effort to a privileged few.

A "growth mindset" however, thrives on challenge and doesn't see failure as an example of unworthiness, but as an opportunity for growth and contribution. These two mindsets are adopted from a young age and play a big part in our attitudes and perceptions of success and failure, and ultimately our capacity for fulfillment.

How people interpret challenges or criticism is a personal choice. We can see them as signs of our unworthiness or weaknesses, or take on a growth mindset and invest more time on reflection, updating strategies, increasing effort, and truly expanding our abilities. We can learn to appreciate the lessons and enjoy the journey as we progress.

Marianne Williamson states, "Our deepest fear is not that we are inadequate, our deepest fear is that we are powerful beyond measure."

Is the fear of the unknown, the fear of change, or the fear of rejection or success scaring you away from your vision, and ultimately your fulfillment?

It is important to become aware of how we are negatively sabotaging our success. The language in which we speak to ourselves, and the words that we use, can determine precisely how we feel at any given point in time, and what we feel can determine the way we behave, and how we behave can create and draw our experiences.

It is the law of attraction; what we create in the form of thoughts and words, creates our version of reality. It is our world, our view of it and subsequently becomes true for each of us.

Someone who is happy and successful in life is completely aware of the language they use. They refuse to indulge in negative self-talk and continuously progress towards their vision and a successful future.

So next time you find yourself moving away from your vision for success, here is a simple technique for changing the negative vibe to a more positive one:

1. Notice the thought and write it down.
2. Next to the negative thought, write down the opposite thought. For example, if the negative thought pattern is, "I am too dumb to do this, there are plenty of others who are more qualified than me", the opposite would be something like "I am proud of who I am and what I've accomplished. I am grateful for my own capabilities and uniqueness."
3. Pause, breathe and connect. Feel truly grateful for this reminder and consciously fill your heart with love and kindness.
4. Write down all your past experiences that support and validate the new positive thought.

"We cannot solve our problems with the same thinking we used when we created them." ~ Albert Einstein

Whatever journey we choose to embark upon, it is vital to keep an open mind so that we can recognize opportunities and take advantage of them.

Choose to persevere with your visualizations, day after day, with patience, dedication and faith. It is never about the results you achieve, but more about enjoying the process of dreaming and taking action. It truly works for the people who believe in the journey more than the goal.

Begin with these three pillars of success. Build a compelling vision of your future – one that consistently inspires and motivates you. Build your resources and empower yourself towards a bright and supported future. And lastly, build your mindset so that when emotional or circumstantial pitfalls do present themselves, you can jump over them with surety, confidence and ease.

Divya Bannerjee

About the Author:

Divya Bannerjee began as a Software Engineer and worked as a technology IT Manager for several years. Her quest for the answers to life and it's mysteries drove her to world renowned life success coach and motivational speaker, Anthony Robbins, and teacher and psychologist Cloe Madanes, under whom she was certified to become a Strategic Interventionist.

Divya is also a certified NLP Practitioner, and part-time blogger. Her ultimate goal is to empower women so that they can take back control of their lives and move towards a compelling future. This is her passion and her strength.

Divya spends her time still working part-time in Information Technology, but also runs her own life coaching business for the remaining days of the week.

Her weekends are spent with her family, including a wonderfully kind husband, and two beautiful children. She is on a constant journey to find out more about life and it's lessons, and empowers and inspires women daily through her company Awaken The Inner Goddess.

Unlock Your Personal Power
4 Keys to Create Success through Personal Leadership

"Success is being able to consistently achieve your desired objectives in all areas of life that you value"
- Jack Canfield, Leading Success Coach (USA)

It all starts with you
Here's a story I came across while at school. A farmer lived in his country farmhouse and was a proud owner of a horse. He loved his horse and took good care of it. Everyday, he used to take the horse to a pool near its stable so it could drink and nourish itself. However, in spite of taking the horse to the pool, the horse often had other ideas. It would play around the pool, sit there and rest, but not drink. The farmer often coerced the horse to drink, but it wouldn't budge. And then, there were times in the day when the horse used to walk to the pool by itself and drink water. The farmer quickly came to the realisation that no matter what he did, it is the horse who decides whether to have water, and left it at that. I guess this is the story where the famous quote came from- "You can take the horse to the water, but cannot make it drink"!

In life, with our ventures, we are often defined by what we accomplish, the results we achieve. We often observe some people to be considered more successful than others. Some people tend to do ok, and some people barely make it. Here's a thought: If we are defined by our success, what defines success? Here's my take: just as whether the horse drunk water or not depended on the horse, your success depends on one person, and one person only: You.

A very simple version of success is achieving what we want in life. Yet, in our quest to achieve our objectives, we often come across challenges that prevent us from doing so. We then start counting external factors as vital to our success. Other people, certain situations, luck become part of the recipe for success. Interestingly, people who have been successful go through their fair share of challenges and obstacles. Yet, how is it that they attract more success? Simply put, they follow a different recipe- they consider themselves pivotal to their success. Regardless of what else happens around them, they keep going and back themselves to achieve their goals.

A classic scenario of varying levels of success is where 100 students appear for an examination. Most of them pass the examination, some do not. However, only a handful of students form the Top 10 percentile, and distinguish themselves from the rest. Consider this- same situation (examination), same set of challenges (the question paper), yet 10 students succeed better than the remaining 90. It's what they bring to the table that distinguishes successful students from others. Similarly, in a larger context, it's what successful people demonstrate consistently that puts them in a different league- their personal power.

Invoking your Personal Power- The 4 Keys
So we saw that your success relies on yourself, and successful people keep going at it regardless of their circumstances, and demonstrate personal power consistently. What really is personal power? In my words, personal power is your ability to demonstrate self-leadership to achieve your desired objectives. Through self-leadership, you allow yourself to rise above your circumstances and achieve success. This gives YOU the power over your circumstances. So rather than feel powerless against any obstacles, challenges and setbacks, you are empowered to make your way forward.

Curiously enough, personal power is something that we all have. It isn't a special gift that a select few have. What distinguishes successful people from others is their choice to consistently invoke their personal power. How do they do that? This chapter looks at 4 keys that successful people use, and so can you, to invoke their personal power and make success their reality. The 4 keys are given below:
-   Take 100% Responsibility of your Life
-   The Power of Rituals
-   Honour your commitments
-   The game of perseverance and consistency

Take 100% Responsibility of your life
A pair of twin boys was raised by an alcoholic, abusive father. Life was tough, as they barely made their ends meet due to the man's constant drinking habits. Very little attention was given to the twins' development as their father himself was unable to fend for himself. Over the years, one of the twins grew up to be a very successful businessman, well regarded in society. The other twin grew up to be just like his father- miserable, alcoholic and struggling to make ends meet.

The media followed the successful twin brother, and came to know about his brother. Curious as to how two brothers can have such contrasting ways of living, they conducted an interview of both brothers separately. One of the questions asked in the interview, and a very key question was "What do you believe to be the biggest reason for your current situation?" Pat came the reply from both brothers, "With a father like that, what else would I have done?"

Same environment, same upbringing, same set of challenges. How is it that instead of ending up similarly, one brother found his way and created success? While the other just fell victim to his circumstances? The successful brother choose to exert his personal power, rather than let his environment control his fate. He did so by taking 100% responsibility of his life.

When you take 100% responsibility of your life, you own everything that goes on- the decisions you make, the actions you take. When you take ownership of your thoughts and actions, you also take ownership of the results that follow. People who take 100% responsibility do not blame others or their situations when things don't go as planned. Instead, they choose to focus on what they can do differently next time, so that they get better results. People who tend not to take 100% responsibility often indulge in blame game, denial, finding excuses. For them, their success is based on external factors. If those factors don't align, they tend to go nowhere.

Being a huge sports fan, I often like to follow the post-game conversations of my favourite sports. Basically, the ones where the players are interviewed for their thoughts on the results of the game. Those conversations reveal the true character of champion sportspersons. I often find that the most successful players, the champions take 100% responsibility for their results.

If they lose, especially due to a bad decision, or someone else's fault (in a team game), they choose not to blame those factors. Instead, they accept the result, and focus on what they could do better next. Sure enough, they come back stronger, and claim the victory they deserve. It's interesting to notice the difference in their attitude, and results with those players who play the victim card. Believe me, there can be lots of sore losers in sports!

How do you know if you are taking 100% responsibility of your life? Think of scenarios in your life, either in personal or professional ventures where things do not go as planned, or you do not get a positive outcome. What do you focus on? Do you focus on how your environment or your situation played a part in those results by forcing your hand? Or do you focus on how you can prepare yourself and do things better for next time? And this gets even cooler, whichever choice you make, do you feel powerless or powerful?

The Power of Rituals
Generally speaking, our life includes 4 key areas:
- Physical
- Mental
- Emotional
- Spiritual

We tend to have activities and goals around each of the above areas. You can also say that each of these areas represent different needs that we might have. When all of these needs are met, and we are able to focus on all 4 areas, our quality of life gets enhanced. How specifically? Here's an example- often, people who seem to be very successful professionally, often complain or lament about the fact that they do not get enough family time or time to take care of themselves? While their mental needs are met (at work), their emotional (family time) and physical/spiritual (time for self) needs aren't getting met. Over time, this starts to reflect on their performance at work as well.

If we do not focus on a certain area of our life, there tends to be pressure built up in that area. Almost like a pressure tank. As we neglect this further, the pressure keeps on mounting. This then causes us stress, and limits us from achieving our goals in that area, as well as other areas in life. Going by the definition of success I shared at the beginning of the chapter, people who are truly successful tend to balance all 4 areas in life very well, thereby meeting their needs and limiting the stress across each area. How do they do that? One word answer: Rituals.

What is a ritual? A ritual is something you do regularly and consistently. Simple examples of rituals could be your morning walk, reading a book everyday, morning tea at work, or Friday night Movies and Pizza with family. So how do rituals help you with your balancing act? By following a ritual in a particular area of your life, your needs there are met. Basically, you start filling up your pressure tank in that area with the rituals you perform. As you do that, you build your endurance by cutting off the area of pressure. When you build your endurance, you are in a great position to tackle any challenge that comes up in that area.

Let's pick one of the examples to illustrate this. Say, you have a ritual of pizza and movies with your family every Friday night. By following this ritual, you are able to spend quality time with your family. Now, let's say you have a challenging week at work which causes you to work long hours during the week. This has potential to throw your work-life balance out of sync. However, since you know that come what may, you are spending Friday night with your family, you do not let your work challenges affect you. If at all, you get an added motivation to handle those challenges knowing you have the certainty of Friday night.

Let's now consider what if there was no Friday night ritual? Not rosy at all, right? Because our emotional needs are taken care of, any challenges that come up in our environment, we tend to handle them well. You will find that as you perform more rituals across every area, you feel more content. This builds your endurance levels. Any setbacks, any challenges can be dealt with better and you seem to have all the power in the world against unforeseen circumstances. This is what successful people do so well. They fill their day or week with rituals across some or all 4 areas to build their endurance. And that's their secret of having it all together when challenges come up.

What rituals do you perform in each of the 4 areas? If not, what can you start following? Remember, whatever ritual you pick, can be the simplest of activities. It does not have to be an elaborate task. If you do perform any rituals, how helpful do you find them in building your endurance?

Honour your commitments
A senior manager in a company was faced with a decision to promote one of his subordinates for a higher role. He narrowed his selection down to 2 candidates, who were equally competent and knowledgeable in their field of work. He made his decision, and conveyed the same to the executive management for their approval. The executive management were keen to know who would be selected, as the role in question was an important one.

One of the executive managers asked the senior manager the rationale for his decision, as both candidates were closely matched. The senior manager replied "While both of them have an equally good profile, my decision came down to one thing. The candidate I selected has always kept his promise, even for the smallest of things. Whatever he commits to, he delivers, even if he has to go out of his way." He continued "With the other candidate, I have often experienced scenarios where he hasn't kept up with his promise to some of his team members, and they have had to wait while he delivered. With such an important role, I know I can trust the candidate I have chosen as what he promises, will be delivered as required, when required".

Isn't it interesting that the criteria for selection between 2 individuals came down to something that was beyond technical capability? The successful candidate demonstrated something the other didn't- honouring his commitments. Why was that deemed so vital? When we honour our commitments, we gain immense trust and credibility from others. We are perceived as reliable. When people perceive us as reliable, they trust us with the important stuff and take us more seriously.
This healthy perception allows us to create functional, healthy relationships with others. The best part of the relationship? There's ample amount of trust, brought about by our sincerity to keep our word. And then interesting things start to happen. People look to go out of their way to honour their commitments just as we do. We become influencers in our community, and that is a hallmark of successful people. Through their behaviour, successful people demonstrate a high standard, which people look to emulate. This is personal power at its inspiring best.

Think of someone you know in your personal circle or at work, who is known to honour his/her commitments. How differently do you perceive them as against someone who barely keeps their word?

There might be the odd occasion where we may not be able to honour our commitment. Would that impact our trust and credibility? If such a scenario occurs, the best approach would be to let the others know at the earliest that you won't be able to deliver what you committed, and indicate the earliest possible time by when you can. In moments like these, it's all about taking 100% responsibility for not being able to deliver as promised, and making sure you deliver by the revised time.

The Game of Persistence and Consistency
An elderly man moved to a farmhouse in the countryside to spend his retirement days. One fine morning, he noticed a young man walk by the house with a shovel in his hand. He made his way towards the nearby fields, and disappeared by a clump of trees. The elderly man saw the young man walk by every day, at the same time and used to disappear by the trees. This went on for a week. He then became curious. "I've got to find out what this young man does, where does he disappear every day", he thought.

The next day, he went to the clump of trees where the young man used to disappear by, waiting for the young man. Right on cue, the young man arrived. "Young man", he asked, "I have been noticing you at the same time every single day. Where do you go to every day?" The young man replied without hesitation, "Come along sir, I'll show you".

The young man led the elderly person to a nearby field. In the centre of the field, there was a long trench that was dug out. Looking at the trench from left to right, the starting end of the trench was dug very shabbily. As the trench moved to the centre, the quality of the digging improved slightly, but still looked like it needed improvement. As the trench moved to the end, the quality improved immensely, and looked like a perfectly dug trench.

"What's this about?", the elderly person asked. The young man explained, "Sir, I recently got a job as a trench digger at a nearby site. I do not have any experience of digging trenches. So that I can get some practice and keep my job, I come here everyday to dig a trench. At first, it was a massive struggle for me, and I did an awful job. As I kept practising, I got more comfortable with this, and the quality of my digging improved. I can now effortlessly dig a trench, and very neatly at that. Yesterday, I got hired as a permanent employee in recognition of my good work". "Well done, what's next", the elderly man asked further. "Just keep coming back, and practice to improve my skills", the young man smiled.

There is a quote that comes to my mind every time I go through this story. Persistence gives you what you want, consistency allows you to keep it. The young man started off without any experience of digging trenches. However, he persisted, and as he did that, he got better. Just a thought, had he not persisted with his practice of digging trenches, would he have gotten better? And once he started getting used to digging trenches, he consistently practiced. Again, if he had not shown consistency, would he have reached the standard required to keep his job?

People who succeed in their ventures have a knack of persisting with what they believe is right. If it is an unfamiliar to them, it may seem like a struggle at first, as the young man found out. However, by persisting, the unfamiliar becomes familiar. As they demonstrate consistency, the familiar integrates into their comfort zone. This is the game of persistence and consistency, where anything can be achieved, as long as you keep playing the game.

We all have played this game at some stage in our lives. A simple example would be learning to drive a car. When you started to learn, how bumpy was the ride? Did it feel comfortable? Yet, as you persisted, what happened? The ride became less bumpy. As you consistently practiced your driving skills, you become good at it, and earned your driving license.

It keeps getting interesting. As we do things on a consistent basis, we become better at what we do. As we become consistent, we become a symbol of certainty. Often, in challenging situations, the people who demonstrate consistency of behaviour and actions are the ones who others look up to. They are the ones who can be trusted to deliver when things appear bleak. Even with the other keys to personal power, our success is determined by how consistently we follow those. Simply put, consistency is one of the attractive qualities of a human being.

In your ventures, think of scenarios where you demonstrated perseverance and consistency. How did you experience growth when your demonstrated these qualities?

In Summary...

We all have access to our personal power. How consistently we tap into it, determines the level of success that we can achieve. The 4 keys shared in this chapter help you create success in your ventures by claiming your personal power. In doing so, you become the leader that inspires others. Here's to unlocking your personal power, and your success!

Arpan Roy

About the author

Arpan's purpose as a leader is to inspire others to realise their peak potential. He has a corporate background with proven experience of leading teams of 20 or more spread across multiple locations. Arpan has extensive experience in managing team dynamics, analysing and solving problems, and mentoring team members to make them better leaders. He also has detailed experience in running and facilitating workshops to enable various stakeholders to reach their desired outcomes.

During his corporate career, Arpan recognised the value of leadership and the satisfaction he got by inspiring others to perform at their highest potential. This inspired him to start his business in Leadership Consultancy and Training called Arman Consultancy. Through his business, he collaborates with leaders in business to define productivity and profit and achieve accelerated business growth. Some of the key problems he addresses for his clients is lack of team engagement, low productivity, culture of reactive thinking within the team, and lack of clarity on how to inspire the team to realise their potential and seek growth.

Arpan specialises in various methodologies such as Values Pendulum®, Neuro-Linguistic Programming (NLP) and Deep State Repatterning®. Using these, he identifies the cause of unrealised individual performance and business growth and creates effective and sustainable models for change that empower his clients to achieve the desired results.

In addition to his corporate background, Arpan is also an MBA graduate, and has detailed understanding of key business functions, which enables him to assist his clients more effectively.

If you are curious how you can achieve business growth through effective leadership in your organisation, you can contact Arpan at:

arpan@armanconsultancy.com.au or +61414274812.

10 Steps To Reinvention In The 21st Century

Ageism is alive and well in Australia and in many other parts of the world.
Under 25's have huge problems finding work, as they need University degrees and recent qualifications to get to an interview, yet they have few opportunities to gain experience.
At the other end of the equation comes the over 50's. In recent times, the Federal Treasurer has kindly informed Australians that we need to work until we are 70 years of age. Given that we have an ageing population which is living 15 to 20 years longer than we were 50 or 60 years ago, that seems to be a reasonable comment on the surface. The reality is significantly different.
Between 2%-3% of the Australian workforce goes through some form of redundancy, retrenchment or forced change of employment circumstances in any year. Many of those people are those over 45, in a disproportionately high representation of the overall group. There are numerous reasons why companies go through retrenchment processes, however the question is why are older people particularly disadvantaged?
Are we suddenly lazier? Are we unable to change? Are we unable to provide good value to business? Are all our skills and expertise suddenly no longer relevant? Are we not pretty enough to make the business look good?
There is a whole range of questions that will never be answered because of political correctness. That is a whole debate on its own. The unavoidable truth is that this happens, and there are any number of politically correct answers to be given as to why a person over the age of 50 may not be given an equal opportunity.
Experienced people who lose employment over 50 years of age have the grim reality that they will have an average of 15 months out of work, and after 2 years unemployment they have a very slim chance of any possible employment unless they create their own opportunities.

Reinvention is the answer!
How do you go through the process of reinventing and rejuvenating yourself when you are in the latter part of your working life? Let us start the process.

1: Make a List of Your Experience

When you have lived to 50+ years of age you have done quite a few things in life. You may have married, raised children, possibly divorced, worked in several jobs and different occupations, participated in sport, social clubs, performed charity work and a thousand other experiences.

Remember that every one of your experiences in life forms part of your resume. It is not all about just what you have done in employment. Working for money is just part of your experience in life. Don't look on yourself as "Just a washed-up (*fill in your job title here*) worker". It is all just a matter of perspective and you are an expert in many things. You may not really see it immediately, but it is true nevertheless.

You are far more than the activities you have undertaken to gain an income through your life. Truly embrace your experiences and look at all the skills required to do any task in life. All skills can be transferred to different areas in life, and in our case we are looking to have a really full view of your individual skill sets so that you can match them in to various opportunities as they arise.

Make a list of the things in which you have experience from jobs to hobbies. The power of making this list is to empower you. As an ordinary father, a job list could include things like husband, father, child minder, lawnmower, gardener, cleaner, carpenter, painter, plumber, taxi driver, carer, cook, sportsman, coach, counsellor, organiser, committee member, wood worker, sailor, salesman, legal expert, trainer, mentor, and a dozen other things.

I would be surprised if you could not find at least 20 things where you have some experience.

Remember, it's not only paid employment where you gain experience.

2: Identify and List Your Strengths

Make a list of your strengths in all the things that you have done in life, and break them down into smaller more specific details.

'Great leadership' may more appropriately be broken into aspects such as 'I am great at managing the team', 'I am great at talking through problems', 'I am brilliant at teaching new team members'.

As a gardener, you may be an expert in orchids and be able to recognise dozens of different types of species of that plant. You may also be good at keeping the lawn in good shape, pruning plants, or be an expert in treating different types of plant diseases. You may be experienced at some basic level of landscaping, have an ability to operate hand tools, push a wheelbarrow, dig holes, and a dozen other things just in that category.

You should be able to have a very extensive list by the time you go through the specifics of each category.

The advantage of making this kind of list is to demonstrate the broad variety of talents and strengths that you have as an individual. You may have worked in the one job for the past 30 years and are feeling really poor after retrenchment, however life has taught you a huge variety of skills.

Sometimes it takes a bump in the road for us to fully appreciate the skill sets that we have developed over a lifetime. This demonstrates the huge "point of difference" that you have from younger people also seeking opportunities in the workforce. Just imagine, some unfortunate 21-year-old may be about to compete with you for employment, yet you will have so many different skill sets and levels of experience that you can sell to your potential employer that it will make any younger person's application look pitiful!

Also speak with your friends and family, and asked them to write a list of the things where they see you having strengths. You may be surprised at what other people see as strengths within you that you may not see yourself!

3: Make a Wish List

Reinventing yourself gives you the opportunity to look at where you REALLY want to be.

We don't often have times in our lives where we make the time to reflect, so make the most of it. You could call it your "bucket list" or whatever name you wish to give it. Everybody I know has dreams, and most people I know have unfulfilled dreams. Many people gave up on their dreams a long time ago, and I have been guilty of that too.

Write down where you want to be in 10 years from a **financial** point of view. Do you want to be retired? Do you want to be independently wealthy, or relying on a pension? Do you want to be living in a better house or downsizing, or moving elsewhere? Where do you want to be living? Do you want to be this living in the same suburb, or do you want to be able to move to a location that that is more suited to the way you wish to live, or the climate that you seek?

Write down where you want to be in 10 years' time regarding your **health**. It may be an opportunity to look at doing something to get fitter, lose a few kilograms, de-stress, reduce blood pressure or any other number of goals. Over the course of a lifetime and as we get older many people have fallen into habits of being less active than is healthy. There are always a few more aches and pains, and it can sometimes be a lot easier to sit down after a hard day's work.

For more mature people, often we are in positions where we are supervising and not as physically active as we used to be in our work life. Many clients have found that when they have a little bit more spare time following retrenchment, it releases them of a lot of workplace drudgery. Some have chosen to go to the swimming pool to do some exercises. Others have walked around their neighbourhood or found walking trails, and many have found that this was really good for their thought processes. Just having a walk for an hour can allow you time to think about your situation. The other bonus was that it could lead to you losing weight and increasing your health!

Write down what you want to be able to do regarding **holidays or adventures** or anything that you really want to do. Do you want to go for that trip to India? Do you want to travel through Europe? Do you want to be sailing around the South Pacific? Do you want to go skydiving?

Write down the list kinds of things to which you want to **contribute**. Do you want to help establish schools in disadvantaged parts of the world? Do you use want to sponsor a child overseas? Do you want to donate to your local church? Do you want to do volunteer work in local or remote communities? Let your imagination go wild!

Also write down where you want to be in your **relationships**. For some of this this can be a very sobering exercise, however it is still very important and can really serve you well.

Relationships take many forms. You may be a couple without kids, a blended family, single and wanting a relationship, or single and happy being that way! At a time of reinvention it is important to evaluate every aspect of our lives and where we are heading. Let's face it, we are in a situation where our life is being forced to change, however life always changes whether we want it to or not!

In 10 years' time (hopefully) you and other people in your life are likely to be in a completely different phase of your lives. If you have another person sharing your life now, how do you want the future to look with your relationship?

If you have children, it is possible that they may be in the throes of independence or even starting their own family. What sort of relationship you want to have with your children? Will they be married and having children? Will they be building their first home? Where is it likely that they will be living? Do you want to be living near them, or further away? What sort of relationship you want to have with your grandchildren?

When you go through each of the different categories you will find that you are able to get some clarity about where you want to be in 10 years' time, and this will give you some place to start planning ahead for a spectacular future.

4: Get Your Body Moving!

I know that it sounds like I'm trying to turn you into a new person. Hmmm...maybe there is some truth in that! Let's face it, most of us need to get a little bit more active!

Have you ever found that after years of working, coming home tired and putting your feet up you had put on weight, had elevated blood pressure and the usual "middle age spread"? It's one of those things about getting older where our experience in our previous work may have led us to supervisory roles which are less physically challenging. They are no less mentally tiring, but the physical side may have decreased.

You don't have to be some new age fitness freak and devote your life to getting fit and eating tofu unless that is what you really want for yourself. If you do – fine, but for the majority of us that is often too hard to think about. Many people faced with the need to reinvent themselves can be going through a mental battle. It is likely that they will be feeling poor mentally, and the motivation to get up to do anything else is all too hard. It is really easy to sit in front of the television or read newspapers and tune out to the world. The danger is that by doing nothing, we only make the situation far worse.

I suggest that you go for a walk. It doesn't matter if you go for 500 metres or 5 kilometres. You don't have to become an athlete, but getting out will give you huge advantages physically and mentally. The health experts all agree that getting a 15-30 minute period of physical exercise per day can decrease the incidence of health issues significantly.

Walking gives you time to think, breathe a bit of fresh air and gives you some space mentally to chew through ideas or issues.

You don't have to power walk or make a race of it, however the act of walking actually pumps your body muscles and in particular your lymphatic system which helps to clear your body of toxins. Sitting around just allows the toxins in the body to build up as they do not get moved through the body system.

When you have less rubbish floating around in your body system you are able to think better and with more clarity. Your issues will have better time to be resolved mentally rather than stewing on things forever.

An alternative is to go out in the garden if you have one and do a bit of weeding for 30 minutes, or walking to the shop to get the milk.

It is not hard, and the benefits are huge. Just try it for a week. I have a personal target of 10,000 steps per day, however ANY movement is good. There are a large number of apps that you can download free to your mobile phone to count your footsteps each day, and several different devices on the market if you want to go to that expense.

5: Get Real

It is time to get real. Seriously.

This can be an emotional time, and I assure you that in times of vulnerability and uncertainty come our greatest learnings. Prepare yourself. You will need to get real about your situation, yourself, and the way you do things.

One of the huge issues with reinvention is that often we have to step outside our comfort zone. Staying in that comfort zone is not an option if you need to reinvent yourself. It is not only for people over 50, but for any person who is in a group which has a disadvantage. Overcoming that disadvantage requires some form of reinvention, or at the very least a different way of looking at the problem. If you identify yourself by your problem, you're never going to get out of it. People like Nick Vujicic (who was born without arms or legs) are great examples of people who have had what many of us consider to be a massive disadvantage, yet have gone on to live fantastically productive lives.

It is okay to feel frightened, uncertain, and vulnerable. This is the time when you will possibly feel all those emotions yet it will all help to get the mental juices flowing. The trick is not to allow your imagination to run away with a negative mindset. It is very simple to find yourself unemployed, and then become a slave to those fears.

As an example, it is a natural and normal reaction to have a fear that you will not have any possibility of getting new employment. It is a possibility which would have significant consequences if it were true. IT IS ONLY A FEAR, IT IS NOT REALITY.

If you allow your imagination to become a slave to that fear you will be increasingly fearful, looking at all the possible "what if" scenarios and becoming locked in sadness and depression. The by-product of that thought process is that you become locked into being sad and negative which will interfere in any attempts to gain employment. If you were an employer offering a job and somebody who was obviously sad, stressed and depressed arrived at an interview do you think they would be an attractive candidate?

To get real, you need to have courage to find the actual truth of a situation. In this example, the actual truth is that you may not be able to find new employment immediately, however if you channel your energy into finding other employment opportunities eventually it will happen. Even if it is charity work, volunteering for local services or other similar activities, it is all employment. It may not pay well or at all, but it is still employment.

To channel your thought processes into dealing with the actual reality of your situation rather than running away with the fears can be a challenge. A grounded way of thinking will be far more beneficial than allowing the fear and uncertainty run away with your mind.

It is an interesting challenge to maintain a grounded way of thinking, yet allow yourself the creative possibilities of creating a new life.

6: Set a Goal and Make a Plan

To re-inventors, having a goal to work towards is the quickest way of gaining momentum and moving forward. There are a few criteria that you need to know when setting a goal so that it becomes a reality. The simplest method is to create what are known as SMART goals.

Specific: It is important to be specific, and not general when setting a goal.

Measurable: Your progress should be measurable.

Achievable: Break the ultimate goal into "bite-size" chunks. Achieve one chunk and then go for the next one, rather than trying to do everything at once. By gradually stretching your comfort zone you can gain more and more momentum.

Realistic: The goal must be realistic. If it is too small, it lacks impact. If it is too big you may be setting yourself up to fail.
Timely: You must be able to measure it in a time period.

For example, your outcome may be to lose some excess weight.

Initially I set a goal like "I want to lose weight". Is it possible that this goal lacks a certain amount of enthusiasm? It is only a general goal, and not very specific.

There is no measurement to the progress, and it is only vague and unstructured so therefore not really achievable. It gives no "Oomph"! There is no pathway to make it realistic, and there is no time defined. It also focuses on "LOSING" which the human brain actually avoids, and focuses on the "WEIGHT". This is actually a plan likely to fail, and one of the reasons that weight loss goals often end up with yo-yo results!

By just making a couple of alterations, we can get some real positive movement in this person's reinvention. If I was to change the goal to "I focus on eating a healthy diet and weigh "x" kilograms by "date"" then we have a positive goal, specific in the detail. It is measurable, achievable, realistic and with a committed timeline.

Weight loss is only an example. The same principles can be applied to any goal involving reinvention. It may involve things including family, finances, health, business, new opportunities, writing a new book, developing an e-business or 1000 other ideas.

Whatever you need to achieve your goal be it money, time or effort, at least you have an idea of what it will take. It is important to impress upon you that it is an important part of the reinvention process.

Once you have defined the goal, then you can set up a plan to achieve the outcome. The plan is a series of steps to get to where you want to go. For instance, using the above example we can take some steps such as:

1: Set up an eating plan.
2: Make a chart to measure the weight loss progress.
3: Place an alarm in your telephone to remind you to weigh yourself on Monday mornings.
4: Clear your cupboard of things that do not fit into your eating plan.
5: Commit to walking 30 minutes every day.

To actually have a concrete, definite plan is a really cool place to be when you are faced with a lot of uncertainty.

7: Work the Plan

Taking action on your plan is the first step. Followed by the second step. And the third step, and so on. To reinvent yourself you must take steps towards your target.

There is no substitute for action.

Like most people, I have had some lofty goals from time to time, many of which have not been achieved. The truth is, I didn't take effective action towards those goals. I had some "airy fairy" ideas, but I did not break them down into the steps I needed to take to reach those goals. The steps looked too big.

I was reminded recently by a friend that any goal was possible. He asked me, "How do you eat an elephant? The answer: One mouthful at a time!" The whole point is that it didn't matter how huge the goal may seem at the start, by taking single steps towards achieving the goal, anything is possible.

Going through reinvention means that we have to have some goals, and plan a pathway towards those goals. By having a commitment to work the plan, we are able to take steps toward their ultimate goal.

The sports apparel company Nike have what I think is the best corporate motto: "Just Do It". If you choose to "Just Do It" for yourself, the results may be spectacular!

JUST TAKE THE CHANCE!

8: Sell Yourself

The path of reinvention can be difficult if you don't learn how to sell yourself. When we have years of experience or see ourselves as one particular thing, it can be easy to fall into the trap of failing to see what other people see. You may be an experienced person and an expert in your field. It is obvious to everyone you have worked with in the past.

Reinvention can be scary because it means that we have to start from the ground floor. It can seem like a lot of hard work and effort when you have spent your life getting to this space, only to find that you need to reinvent yourself. If you want to change, you have to take on new ideas and new values.

How comfortable are you going to feel if you _don't_ reinvent yourself? You may be stuck in a rut of the rest of your life, and where is the fun in that? I have seen people who at 50 are useful and invigorating, and great people to be around because they look forward to tackling new challenges in whatever aspect of life comes up. I have also seen people who are tired, worn out and old simply because they think that way.

To be positive can be a bit confronting, so I suggest that <u>before</u> you make a telephone call or make contact with people, SMILE! In the mirror at home, in the car or wherever. Smiling actually relaxes your face but importantly it will place you in a more positive frame of mind.

Jump up and down on the spot and do something to raise your energy levels before you go in to start talking. I know that sounds insane but it actually works! Just try it and see!

9: Don't Be Afraid of Rejection

The huge advantage that older people reinventing themselves have is that they have learned about resilience. It is something that is only learned through experience, and a cornerstone of reinvention.

If you are looking for in a new job, expect to have many of your attempts to apply for positions to be ignored or unsuccessful. After all, you only need ONE successful application!

I have heard of stories of thousands of applicants for one position, and that means that all except one have been rejected. Get over yourself and get on to the next one if a job is all that you are chasing!

Remember that success in all sorts of things is learned. You are perfectly capable of learning anything, and the more you practice the better you will get! If you do your research, find the needs of the prospective employer, new business, new pathway forward in your life to seek spiritual enlightenment or whatever your cause, you increase your opportunities to reinvent yourself by accepting rejection and learning from it.

If you choose to start your own business or whatever course of life you choose, remember that you will still face rejections at times. Just be aware that it happens, and if you don't take it personally then the next opportunity will arise very quickly, and usually it will be better anyway!

10: Be Grateful

I suspect that I know what you're thinking about now...

If someone had told me to be grateful for being forced into life-changing circumstances, made redundant, retrenched, or forced to retire when I didn't want to - I would probably have thought they were right off their trolley.

The power of gratitude is important if you want to reinvent yourself.

Be grateful for the friendships you have developed, your family, your children, the opportunity to feed and educate yourself and any family you have, the lessons learned, the health that you have - all the positives that may exist.

The important thing about finding gratitude in your darkest hour is that you will be actually tuning your brain into a positive frame of mind. It is also the truth when we find gratitude for all the good things that have happened, more good things will happen to you in the future. I assure you that **if you wake up every day and find 10 things for which you are grateful - your life will transform quickly.**

Every day I am grateful for the joy I have in my relationships, the food on my table, the freedom to do as I please, my health, and 1000 other things. I find that by bringing 10 things to the front of my mind each morning, and saying out aloud "I am grateful for..." it provides me with a huge mental boost.

Anyone can do this stuff. All it takes is a choice.

Your choice.

Do you choose to move on quickly to the next phase of your life with as little emotional baggage as possible, or do you want to become that grumpy old person you never dreamed of becoming?

I do not subscribe to the view that you are washed-up, a has-been, useless, or without value. You have a wealth of talent and knowledge that you can sell. I have never met a person who did not have value in the community. Ever.

Anyone reinventing themselves needs to have the confidence to acknowledge their skills and the value that they have. If you acknowledge those skills and the values that you provide to everybody around you, all you have to do is sell the idea that you will be valuable and an addition to whatever venture you decide to apply yourself to.

Everything in life is ultimately about sales. Know that you are a great product to sell, one you believe in, one that the world has the right to share. It is your duty to yourself and those who love you to be the best you can be.

GO OUT AND GET THE LIFE YOU DESERVE!

Neville Stone

About the Author

Neville Stone is a Business and Life Coach. He has walked the walk of redundancy and retrenchment, and has studied in the personal development field for many years prior to opening his current practice.

Assisting people to reinvent themselves following major events in their lives is his speciality. His coaching focuses on uplifting people from mental states that do not help people move forward, to a place where they are able to prosper. This helps people create new lives, identities and forward movement.

Have you ever felt stuck? Have you been confused and uncertain as to the next step you need to take? Have you ever wondered if what you are going through NOW is all there is? These are the kinds of questions that Neville Stone assists his clients in answering on the pathway to REINVENTION!

Website: www.worldsyourgem.com.au

Email: nev@worldsyourgem.com.au

How To Maximise Your Inner Creative Genius

WE ARE DAMAGED GOODS

Unlike many other attributes that people aspire to, I find that people have fairly extreme views on their own creative ability. When you ask the question 'are you creative?' they tend to put themselves in two camps. The confident-yet-modest "oh yeah I'm quite creative actually" or the dismissive "I'm not creative". The answer comes with no hesitation and the belief is firmly engrained in one's psyche. On further investigation signs point to significant moments or the influence of others in affecting people's creative confidence. We are in effect, damaged goods. Like anybody who has had a bad break-up or been bitten by a ferocious dog, the moment lives with us for a long time and sub-consciously becomes a much bigger event than it actually was.

Creativity is an emotional pursuit where we share a piece of ourselves, and if we don't get the response we want, it hurts. It really hurts. At sixteen I was a prolific songwriter, gigging and recording and loving every moment. At nineteen I joined a very talented group of musicians who were all degree level music students. In one of my first rehearsals with them one of my song ideas was discarded as it wasn't musically 'valid'. It took me at least 5 years to finish writing another song; those darn demons talk loud.

Despite this, in my working life I always had the reputation "Get Matt in. He's fabulous with ideas." I have trained and coached thousands of people in unlocking their own creative ability in my work at the unique and energetic creative leadership specialists, Upping Your Elvis.

Albert Einstein stated that "creativity is just intelligence having fun" and once you get your head around the concept that creativity isn't something you have or you don't, it is easier to find your way along the creative path.

Here are a few tips and provocations on how to do so. But remember, it starts with you and when you find your mojo you won't want to turn back.

THE HARD FACTS

Creativity is a word banded around businesses and sits in many vision and values statements. IBM's global CEO study consistently shows creativity to be the most important leadership attribute. However, the world of business is a daunting place for people to experiment with creativity, the fear of exposing oneself is prolific. The easy route is to follow the norms and the pack. In Adobe's Creativity study 75% of people agreed that creativity is the key to unlocking economic growth. However only 1 in 4 people felt as though they had the permission to be creative in their day-to-day work. Leaders want creative output but value their preconceptions of a 'normal' workplace with people 'looking' busy and efficient, more.

RE-FRAME CREATIVITY

A lot of people put creativity out of reach. Ask them what pursuits they associate with creativity and they will give you answers embedded in their subconscious. Painters, musicians, writers and inventors. Referring to extreme characters in history: Dali, Mozart, Shakespeare and Edison. They often cite other people in the business they work in. The whacky marketing director or the extrovert head of sales, who is just so funny when he presents! Or a link is made to business 'disruptors' such as Uber and Airbnb.

Wooooah. Stop. Don't put too much pressure on yourself!

Creativity can be learnt. The gift that creative people have is their self belief. They are creative because they think they are and are persistent in the pursuit of their dream. Our mind affects how we see ourselves. As a child growing up Pablo Picasso was not seen as having any great artistic talent, he was just encouraged by his artist father to believe that he was. Ray Bradbury set himself a challenge to write one short story every week. In took ten years and 520 stories until he had one strong enough to publish.

Creativity also comes in small moments. We are surrounded with aspirational TV shows like Dragon's Den and listen to TED talks from amazing entrepreneurs who started with nothing, but you don't have to launch the next Spotify in your business to qualify as a creator. Modern society in its state of flux offers endless opportunities to disrupt but in the last half century there has been more value added to businesses through incremental innovation than disruption. Ideas can be simple. A waiter at the Four Seasons hotel group once noticed that it is annoying for guests when you have to keep asking them if they are drinking still or sparkling water when they are topping them up over dinner. So he suggested putting a place mat under glasses containing sparkling water and not under still when the first glass was poured. This way nobody need be disturbed. One of many ideas that make the Four Seasons arguably the best hotel service in the world.

Simple tweaks to business as usual can be highly impactful.

So, knock creativity off its pedestal and find your own language that works for you.

AWARENESS IS KEY

Do you know when you're at your most creative? Where are you and what are you doing? I have asked those questions all around the world and the most popular answers include 'in the shower', 'socialising with friends' or 'driving'. In fact the number one answer in a survey we conducted at Upping Your Elvis was 'in bed'. The least likely place is at your desk. In the words of the American poet Robert Frost "The brain is a wonderful organ; it starts working the moment you get up in the morning and does not stop until you get into the office."

AND SPEAKING OF THE BRAIN

Creative thinking happens when the logical part of your brain (The conscious) can connect with the stimulus store cupboard (The subconscious). Your ability to do that is based on which brain state you are in. At work you spend most of your time in what is known as BETA Brain State. This is when you are busy rushing from meeting to meeting, highly alert, attempting to multi-task and working on different devices. However, your conscious is disconnected from your subconscious and therefore there's NO CREATIVE THINKING HERE! Professor Glenn Wilson, University of London's study at the Institute of Psychiatry suggests that your IQ falls 10 points when you're fielding constant emails, text messages, and calls, the same loss you'd experience if you missed an entire night's sleep and more than double the 4-point loss you'd have after smoking marijuana!

A small proportion of your working day is spent in ALPHA Brain State. This is when you are still very awake but your brain literally relaxes. You aren't quite in a meditative state but it allows deeper creative thinking. You often flip into this unknowingly by going for a cup of tea with a colleague or walking to the printer. However, if you are more aware of the difference between BETA and ALPHA you can deliberately get there yourself within seconds.

Check in with your 'state'. How do I feel right now? Slow Down, sit straight, take 3 deep breaths, smile, unplug yourself from devices and take a walk.

These periods of ALPHA can be extended with practice and we become more able to enter what was researched and theorized in the 1970s by Mihaly Csikszentmihalyi as 'flow'. In an interview with *Wired* magazine, Csíkszentmihályi described flow as "being completely involved in an activity for its own sake. The ego falls away. Time flies. Every action, movement, and thought follows inevitably from the previous one, like playing jazz. Your whole being is involved, and you're using your skills to the utmost."

These ALPHA moments are when our creative juices are quite literally 'flowing'. It maybe a short moment to start but with practice we can retrain our minds with 'state' checking at regular intervals.

SENSITISE YOURSELF – ANSWERS ARE EVERYWHERE!

If you are a purist, everything around you is stimulus that could well be the fodder of your next brilliant creative idea. We often don't know it is there. But just like the fabled Newton and the apple moment, if we are sensitized to what is going on around us then it makes our creative endeavors more effortless. Sir John Hegarty of BBH fame, tells a great tale of his friend Sir Paul Smith waiting on a delayed flight at Milan airport. Everyone "plugs in" to zone out in front of a screen during the wait. Paul, however, decides to take a walk around the airport and check out what is going on. He stumbles upon a lucky charm on the floor which inspires him to use it for a button on a new shirt. The shirt becomes a best seller, selling around 25,000 units. Hence the ownership of his famous strapline 'You can find inspiration in everything, and if you can't look again.'

Just as we are highly susceptible beasties in the eyes of advertisers, with the power of placement and suggestion, we are also highly influenced by our environment and the stimulus it creates. A couple of years ago, Chris Baréz-Brown, the founder of Upping Your Elvis, co-launched a movement called Street Wisdom with fellow creativity guru David Pearl. It is an experience that teaches you how to use your immediate environment to help your answer your life questions. A friend of mine, Scott Morrison, ex commercial and marketing director for Diesel, had a question in his head. "Should I change my career?" Within a 3 hour, highly sensitised experience he found the clarity he wanted to move on, built a proposition for his start-up business and even landed his first client that he happened to meet on the street! Breakthroughs don't happen everyday, sometimes it takes time for the answers to wash over your mind. Scott was in the right 'state' to get creative and allow decisions to become apparent.

Sensitising yourself to your immediate environment involves a process of slowing down –
1. Tune up – slow down, breathe and take time to focus on the details around you.
2. Get clear on a question – once you are close to your question, find a partner and 'talk it out' non stop for 7 ½ minutes (no more, no less, yes that exact time is proven to be the most beneficial!). Your partner will be able to hone in on it more and maybe find a different theme going on.
3. Get Lost – armed with your question, walk and observe detail, allowing your mind to roam and make connections.
4. Feel it, don't think it, we have a tendency to slip into a logical analytical mode and over think. Relax, breathe, smile and see what happens!

CHALLENGE THE DEMONS WITHIN
We all have little voices in our heads. They are primal, part of our caveman DNA and built in negativity bias. Designed to protect us from the next sabre toothed tiger that may approach. We go to an unknown city, turn down a dark alley and the voice will say "Do you really want to go down here?" We then calculate logically what to do next and normally opt for the well-lit street that takes a few seconds longer. Probably a wise choice. But often the little voice in our head can misguide us. It can say things like "that person is out to get you" when really people aren't. Suddenly, we are in a 'road rage' situation, over reacting to a simple event, the actions of human error alone. But why does this happen? Why do we suddenly freak out when somebody forgets to indicate in the car ahead?

Our brains haven't changed anywhere near at the same pace as our environment has. As Dan Gardner explains in his book The Science of Fear "When it comes to the evolution of psychology, we should imagine the development of the human brain by equating the past 2 million years of human development to a 201-page book. Of that book, 200 pages would cover the entire time our species spent being nomadic hunter-gatherers in the Stone Age. The last page would cover our time as an agrarian society. The last paragraphs on the final page would cover the last two centuries of the world we now live in. We are cavemen."

So, that little voice inside isn't always on your side, it can be a demon stuck in caveman times, filled with fear about where that sabre toothed tiger is heading next. We need to tame him and use his resources in emergencies only when we really do need his skillful reactionary efforts.

For example, you have a moment of inspiration at work and you're just about to share it and your demon may say "Is that really a good idea?" or "you might embarrass yourself if you share that!". At that point, many of us pause, and hold back that piece of potential genius for fear of imagined humiliation.

Get aware of the demons within, challenge them and question whether they are serving or sabotaging you

KEEP IT HUMAN
My work has involved training thousands of people in leading and facilitating creativity.

When people really connect with creativity in the workplace, they realise it's not about processes and tools to follow but about flexibility in what you do and how you do things. There was supposedly a sign outside Albert Einstein's door that said: "Not everything that counts can be counted, and not everything that is counted, counts."

They make the creative experience their own and for many, this unleashes new life in them, adding a string to their bow they didn't know they had. Some people force it too much. They dramatically change their character when they are put in front of a room of people with the job of getting creative. They bring out the Hawaiian-shirt wearing, jazz-hand version of themselves that doesn't seem real. People in the room smell a rat and start to think this is an inauthentic performance. Others put way too much pressure on themselves to be the most creative in the room and have all the ideas.

Creativity is not a show and it's certainly not your job to have all the great ideas. Your job is to create the right conditions for others to unlock their creativity. The best way of doing this is to be more of your weekend self.

If you're a storyteller, inspire people.
If you're a joker, make people laugh.
If you're a stat geek, hit people with some profound numbers.

Put simply if you emanate an authentic, engaged, relaxed state and enjoy yourself, everyone else will feel it. This is when the magic will happen. You are in ALPHA state and so are the group you are working with.

To win we have to embrace humanity, it is people alone who choose to realise their creativity. They are the disruptors. Simple, but true.

STRUCTURE IS THE FRIEND OF FLAIR

Now this may seem to jar with my previous point about being human but creativity at work needs a fair bit of rigour. I once went on a week-long tour behind the scenes of organisations famous for everyday creativity such as Innocent Drinks, The Four Seasons and Love Film. Half way through the week one of the group exclaimed "these places have a lot of structure in place to support creativity". They do, they have systems and clear roles where any creative insight or idea can be carefully curated. It's important to have your mini system, your own series of rules by which you operate creatively.

1. Are you crystal clear on the brief or problem at hand?
2. What perspectives do you have from inside and outside the business?
3. Do you know which ideas will be in and out of scope?

The most important structure is the way you set up any meeting or interaction requiring creativity. I was once training a group of very bright young things from one of the coolest media owners in the world, Spotify. Half way through the workshop they realised that the way they could improve their collaborative interaction was through just a little more discipline. They saw their ideas sessions as a bit too kickabout.
They questioned: Who's facilitating? What's the context of the brief? How do you want people to behave, thinking expansively about possibilities or in a reductive more analytical manner?

However, the environment needs to be set up so that it doesn't feel like a regular meeting room space, it is relaxed and informal. Then you can help trigger people's Alpha state. This is why creative businesses such as Google and Pixar are so keen on creating interesting, informal and relaxed workspaces, so people feel free to express themselves and their ideas and that demon takes some time out.

Constraints can go a long way. As the eminent designer Charles Eames said "Design depends largely on constraints." It's the tight and loose of creativity.

Well planned interactions allow people to think "I'm in safe hands" and allow their flair to fly.

PERSONAL PET PROJECT

No matter how fascinating your job is, after a period time it will feel routine.

The human brain will unconsciously develop short cuts in the way we operate. One reason why is because our brain is "inherently lazy" and will always "choose the most energy efficient path" if we let it, writes Tara Swart, a senior lecturer at MIT, in her book *Neuroscience for Leadership*.

The human brain is around 3% of people's body weight but uses 20-25% of our daily energy supply, regardless of what the brain is doing. The more we think, the more energy we use. Kids learn quickly because the brain is still developing and is uber flexible.

Deborah Ancona, a professor of management and organizational studies at MIT explains

"It turns out that we, as human beings, develop neural pathways, and the more we use those neural pathways over years and years and years, they become very stuck and deeply embedded, moving into deeper portions of the brain," she tells *Fast Company*. By the time we get to the age of 25, we just have so many existing pathways that our brain relies on, it's hard to break free of them.

To be creative we have to break our habits but there is no reason to when things are chugging along just fine. Why change what ain't broken? My advice would be to always have a pet project on the go.

Famous stories from much-lauded organisations show that this is best practice. Google allow their engineers 10% of their time at work to meddle with projects that interest them. This allowance of time has led to the creation of Streetview and Google Earth. We can all do that. Whether it's enrolling for a cooking course or setting up a sideline online business selling art we will keep our brain open to new possibilities and it keeps us creatively sharp.

My friend and Elvis partner, Jim, is currently one of 10 guys who have set up a campaign to raise awareness and money for stem cell research. They are doing this by swimming 155 miles down the River Thames but to stand out from the crowd they are only swimming doggle paddle. In 2 months they built an [incredible website](#), launched an app, have a full social media and PR campaign behind them. Although Jim is slightly shattered from doggy paddle training I have never seen a more bouncy, alert man who is learning so much he can apply back to our business.

I get my fresh perspectives from coaching an NGO (Stir Education) who specialise in helping teachers in underserved areas with innovative approaches to teaching. I have no idea about the regulations and politics surrounding their quest but there is value on both sides of a bit of naivety.

So what's your pet project? It gives you more purpose than just the job you do and also keeps you fresh. Double whammy I would say!

LOSE THE PERFECTIONIST GENE

We live in a world where the word 'perfect' is overly sought after. The perfect marriage, the perfect home, perfect college grades and the perfect dinner party hor d'ouvres. In fact, if we've always succeeded and been top of the class and captain of the sports team, we fear what being a bit imperfect may look like. However, with creativity, there is no such thing as perfection. As Salvador Dali bluntly put it "Have no fear of perfection - you'll never reach it." In order to be creative you have to take creative leaps and inherent in that is failure. Your job is then to make sure you learn from those mistakes for next time.

Scott Forstall, who headed up the first iPhone project at Apple talked about always recruiting people with a 'growth mindset' versus a 'fixed mindset'. He wanted to hire people who would swing big, try things and learn quickly, rather than slick perfectionists.

You can achieve this by demanding feedback every day. This is the stuff of the most successful creatives and is also vital for happiness in life.

Laszlo Bock, Head of People Operations at Google in his new book Work Rules! shares how feedback at Google works. "Ask questions, lots of questions. Schedule regular 1:1s with your manager. Get to know your team. Actively solicit feedback-don't wait for it. Accept the challenge (i.e., take risks and don't be afraid to fail … other Googlers will support you). "

So demand feedback every day and take positives on board too. Remember, your demon within (remember his caveman negativity bias?) will only want to hear what you did that was terrible!

Make it human "What did I do well? What could I do even better?"

Remember to ask for specifics rather than generalisations. If somebody says 'you were really engaging', ask what specifically you did that led them to believe you were engaging.

JUMP IN THE DEEP END!

A friend of mine was once in a crisis. She was running a huge awards ceremony for a drinks business and her event photographer pulled out due to illness. On the weekend before she knew I had just bought my first digital SLR camera and so she called me to ask if I could take photos at the event. I laughed and asked how much were they paying for the photographer and she said £1000. Bearing in mind that this was nearly 20 years ago and I had never used a digital camera in my life, this was an audacious or plain silly thing to agree to. But I thought "she needs help so what the hell?". I had done a bit of photography on my degree course with old-fashioned film, so knew enough about composition to get me started, but I needed a bit more swagger to look the part of a pro. I remembered the style of a wedding photographer I had seen in action so I tried on some of his idiosyncrasies for size, I wore all black, shiny shirts, shiny trousers and shiny shoes. I gelled my hair back. I carried a big camera bag, looking like I had a load of kit when in fact, one lens was all I had! I got in people's faces, partied with them using clichés like "make love to the camera". By the end of the evening I thought I had found my calling. The next day I sent the CD off to the client and she called straight back saying they were the best award ceremony photos she's had in years! Now, I know the shots weren't technically brilliant but as I had jumped in and enjoyed it, I had got the most from the people and the situation.

Now, what I am not saying here is change persona. What I am saying is people will spot if you don't fully believe in yourself. And we can never fully believe in ourselves with creativity because it's unknown territory and stuff will go wrong. You will come up with rubbish ideas. But a bit of swagger will carry you through. Just jump in and enjoy but please don't wear shiny trousers!

So those are my tips on how to unlock even more of your natural innate creative genius. As you can see, it is very little about tools and techniques, much more about how you show up. Try some things on for size and see what works for you.

And if you're a boss reading this, creatively confident people are engaged and productive employees.

As McKinsey & Co. partner Michael Rennie pointed out, "What's good for the spirit is good for the bottom line."

I'll step off my soap box now.

Matt Bolton-Alarcón, partner at Upping Your Elvis, specialists in creative leadership.

www.uppingyourelvis.com

About the author

Matt Bolton-Alarcón, Partner, Upping Your Elvis.
www.uppingyourelvis.com

Matt Bolton-Alarcon has travelled a multifarious career path. He has worked as a banker, musician, creative writer, producer, marketing director, trainer, speaker and coach which gave him the knowledge and passion for creativity and innovation. More notably the realisation hit home that he loved generating energy in people and pulling out their creative potential. Matt joined Upping Your Elvis, specialists in creative leadership, as a partner in 2012. Their mission is to help people reconnect with their inner creative genius and become truly confident in who they are. To date they have helped businesses such as Unilever, Diageo, ITV, Nike and Spotify realise their potential: They come back time and again for Upping Your Elvis's unique, refreshing and energetic expertise in fuelling creativity and innovation amongst their teams. Matt is known for his engaging 'wit and wisdom' and has a talent for spotting the hidden potential in individuals as well as helping businesses to get focused on what they really want.

He lives in Sussex with his daughter Frida, wife Delia and dog Taco! They spend many happy and free spirited weekends travelling the countryside in their beloved campervan.

A Non-Negotiable Decision

If I asked you what is success what would you answer?
I am willing to bet that whatever you say will be either an outcome or measure of whether you fulfilled the concept of success. I am willing to go out on a limb and say that whatever explanation you offer of success is a result of success or of adhering to the underlying definition of success but not the very definition of it.
In my early days of going to seminars and workshops I would hear all sorts of explanations about what success is, such as: *its doing what you love, it's having a million dollars in the bank, running your own business, success is a journey (not untrue) and so forth.*
These are all valid answers but what I couldn't reconcile is that there still had to be another level or stage before these in order for these to exist or to be true.
I felt the most common explanations for what success is-was not the definitive definition but outcomes, measures of adherence to success.
Naturally this created a sense of overwhelm in me, especially at this particular time where I was in a bad place and searching for answers.
I really needed an indication of what success was because I desperately needed something positive I could gravitate towards, something that could give me a sense of hope
It was something Tony Robbins said at a seminar of his I went to in 2008 that triggered me to shift my perspective and eventually help me arrive to the true definition, in my opinion of success.
He said ultimately the key to success is taking action, decide and go...It was at that one line I did a double take and began to form my hypothesis and prepare my evidence.
What was my hypothesis, my stunning realisation about what success is?
Quite simply that-"Success is a decision!"
I had chills for this just resonated so powerfully within me, naturally though I thought to myself is that it and if so, how so?
I began to pose the question all these other definitions that have been offered for success, could they have happened without first a decision? For example if a definition for success was to live doing what you love than the

opposite is also possible, in other words it is possible to live doing something you do not feel passionate about, in fact most do.
Which way you go comes down to what you decide to commit to.
This meant that living a life of passion and doing what you love was not success but the result of adhering to a decision.
Even taking action results from deciding to do so, let's take the idea that success is being the best at what you do, let's say that is athletics, to be the best you have to train and eat a certain way, understanding the principle of decision it's also possible to not train in the way that makes you a champion and of course not get the results.
Fundamentally it comes down to your decision and again what you decide to commit to in your life and in all areas of your life.
But is that it? Is it that simple or is there more?
Well it is that simple but there is a little more to it, I began to ask myself is it possible for someone to decide but then at some point to back out?
The answer of course is *yes*, it is possible for someone to commit and then back out so although a decision is the definitive common denominator for success, the decision itself has to be a certain type of decision.
I love hearing stories of people who faced a major adversity and against all natural laws and odds somehow converted that adversity in to great "success".
In all the stories I encountered I noticed, amongst other things, they all shared one major thing, one major factor, that factor is what I call 'The Do or Die Moment'.
The Do or Die Moment is that moment one is made to feel so compelled to make a change or to decide to take certain action because the alternative is death or as good as. The decision in that moment is simply non-negotiable and fulfilling the decision is paramount.
It was here I finally came to the *true definition* of success which simply is
 ……**A Non-negotiable decision.**
WOW! Success is a non-negotiable decision?
Yes, this is precisely what success is, but what does that mean? What do you mean by this Petros?!
Well this definition has a number of insinuations or elements to it, I will explore these for you now to highlight what it means to make a non-negotiable decision……..to Succeed.

Firstly it begins with finding your 'compelling WHY', you see without the right motivation even your decision is a wet cookie tipping over.

Your Compelling WHY......
Many people see the glamorous side or the reward end of achieving in life but are often clueless to the difficulties and challenges that can present themselves along the way.

Many of these challenges can be tough, tedious and time consuming, requiring patience, persistence and sacrifice. If you are to go through that, there'd better be a good reason for it, in fact there would have to be a ' no other option will do' reason to go through the process and challenges. In other words, there has to be a meaningful and compelling purpose to want the final result.

There is an old saying never make a decision when you are really depressed or really excited, the reason for this is you are not in the right frame of mind to make a proper well thought out and certainly non-negotiable decision. Most of all a decision made in either of those extremes is not a decision made with the heart and for true reasons.

This is where so many new-year resolutions begin to go wrong and never get fulfilled, success is a change in lifestyle and thinking, not a flash in the pan idea made under the influence of extreme emotions or distractions like alcohol etc.

It's very hard to decide on something you are not sure about or that isn't something you want or have had a chance to properly weigh up and consider. The 'Why' needs to resonate with you at the deepest level, it needs to be more than an intellectual process or intellectual decision and it needs to be from the heart, from the place of living it and practicality.

When that is formulated then you have all the information and all the true and compelling reasons for taking action, it means then when you finally 'decide' it's based on solid foundations which will hold even when on your journey things go against you, you will have the fuel and motivation you need to keep getting up.

There is going to be many heavy knock downs along the way in being successful, so your 'WHY' must be bigger than each one.

Insistence vs Persistence......
Boy oh boy does this one wreak havoc amongst so many, is it any wonder so many give up so quickly something they swore black and blue was going to be achieved.
How many times have you been told keep at it and you will get there, don't give up, and yet you never got there or became so frustrated you walked away for good?
Wonder why?
So many businesses these days still think it's the 80's and early 90's and so keep doing business or running their businesses the same way they did 30 or so years ago.
They believe if they just open their doors and a good influx of people come in and buy, they will be fine.
They will use low value un-attractive offers and outdated practices and off they go day in day out and every day they wonder why they sit twiddling their thumbs and paying utilities at 2015 rates going broke and yet their competition just a little down the road who has moved with the times is almost having to knock back business.
A little analogy I use, it's a little facetious, is the story Stan. Stan was tasked with bringing water to the village he lived in, as a young man making his rite of passage in to manhood he was proud with the job he was tasked and so off he went.
There were 100 people in the village and all needed water to clean, to wash and to cook so Stan picked up 2 buckets and off he went, 1 kilometer each way to and from the nearest lake filling up the buckets to fill up the local well, it was a scorching day.
The job began to feel tiresome and tedious, a number of the wiser men in the village asked Stan how he was doing and to keep at it. 'I am fine!' he advised, 'I will have water for the village'.
It was getting to lunch time and again the question was asked of Stan, are you coping do you need help, let's have some lunch and we can assist you Stan!
'No no, I'm fine, I can do this, the village will have water', the wiser males looked at themselves and gave a shrug and continued along the day.
Stan would be asked another 4-5 times if he was handling it and if needed some assistance and each time he rejected the offers.

It was finally 6 pm and at this time the villagers would flock to the village well to collect their water for cleansing, cooking and the washing and to the dismay of the village the well was barely half way filled and Stan was still drudging back and forth from the lake, unlikely to finish anytime soon.

Finally one of the village leaders called for Stan's immediate presence and demanded an explanation, 'You were tasked with one job, a job that normally takes others 3 hours approximately and yet today the village is without sufficient water, explain yourself!'

'3 HOURS!!!' exclaimed Stan, 'How is this possible!?'

Because those before you would use one of the horses, tie it up to the town water cart and using the water pump designed to slowly fill it would ensure the town had water.

'But I didn't know we had these tools available?' Foolishly and embarrassed cried Stan.

'That's because you never asked, you decided you were going to do things one way and that way was all there was. You thought you had persistence but instead all you had was insistence and now the town is virtually dry for tonight.'

'It's great you wanted to keep going but you had a choice on how you would go and all you had to do was to take up at least one of the offers for assistance from one of the others and you would have seen a better more efficient way to do your job and progress, even become great at it!'

Does this sound familiar? You see it's a bit of a trap and it's usually our ego that causes us to fall for it because insistence can feel very similar to persistence.

There is however a difference between the two and they are as follows:

Insistence-says that I must force my will or my way, keep doing the same thing and hope somehow I end up with a different more desirable outcome and as good old Einstein points out, that's just insanity. It's the ego looking to satisfy itself and making the situation about itself rather than the greater goal, the greater good being sought.

Persistence-says I don't quit on something worth achieving, I use my outcomes as my guide for what is and isn't working and I use that wisdom to keep adjusting my methods until I achieve my goals.

When you can understand this at the heart level at the doing level and be living it, you will succeed, no doubts about it. It's almost impossible not to.

So this is what it means: **Success is a non-negotiable decision** it's a profound revelation that will alter your life for the better forever once you get it and live it.

Does it end there? Almost, in discovering this magnificent revelation, it gave light to another revelation, a revelation that for all intents and purposes exists for the same above reasons and principles, **can you guess what it is?**

Failure is also a decision, is it non-negotiable? I am undecided because I believe if a person that has resigned to failure can be shown how their goal can be achieved, they may turn on their decision for failure.

You see If success is a decision at the very basic then failure, being the other possibility to success, being the decision to no longer persist with the goal and to walk away, also has to be a decision, because when you aren't deciding for success you are deciding for failure as far as the goal or dream that you were deciding on is concerned.

Why these two revelations are most empowering?

It's very simple knowing that whether we succeed or don't succeed is not controlled by our circumstances but instead us, suddenly we become aware and awakened at how magnificent we are and can be, we realise what beings of infinite possibilities we are.

We begin to see things differently and give new meanings to everything around us which leads to better thoughts and therefore better actions, which ultimately brings us greater results in our life.

You too are that magnificent.......if you decide.

Petros Galanoulis

About the author

Life transition coach supporting and navigating people who are struggling to deal with a major shift/ change in their life such as that experienced from a break up.

From a young age he noticed that people quickly felt comfortable with and found it easy to open up to him. He soon realised he was able to intuitively provide insights and direction beyond his years with significant results.

Based in Melbourne Australia, he works as a life transition coach, predominantly with individuals and entrepreneurs who are struggling to find their footing, sense of direction or purpose after experiencing a major and difficult life transition/ event such as a break up.

Now also works with organisations specifically working with leadership teams to help them be a positive influence and to know what to do when a staff member is experiencing a life difficulty.

With over 15 years of professional experience and over 30 years of personal experience, he developed his coaching process: the G.P.S. system.

Has also studied the spiritual philosophy of Vedanta and is also a Reiki and

Hypnotherapy qualified practitioner and is prolific in NLP, CBT, Narratve Approach, Solution Focused Approach and more.

Petros has appeared in the media and his personal and professional mission is to be constantly looking at and creating different and unique ways to help those who are ready to breakthrough to a life better than they imagined and to inspire them to action and rip off the veil of illusion that is the victim mentality.

Petros is also Co-Owner of I Create Positivity eMagazine, a magazine dedicated to the extraordinary stories and insights of success against the odds from ordinary people in the community together with serving as a platform for professional insights and ideas for personal improvement.

Clients that have worked with Petros have been able to find their purpose or sense of direction and restructure their lives to begin living it authentically, happily and fulfilled.

Petros is also a practical and inspirational speaker and thought provoker.

Voila success.com

The best success books in the world

(Re) Defining Success

What is success? Can you believe that I didn't ask myself this questions until 10 years into striving for it? I spent an entire decade chasing 'success', yet until recently had never taken the time to verbalise what it was for me, what it meant to me, what it looked, felt or smelt like. I hadn't explicitly defined what I would be, have and do once I had achieved it.

Why? Firstly because most people never do, and secondly because I had superficially decided I'd achieved it.

I owned a multi-million dollar business that I'd built single-handedly from the ground up in three different countries, and had 23 staff who loved working with me. I had the beautiful half a million dollar suburban house with a hot tub and swimming pool, the $75,000 car, the nice clothes and an all-year-round sun tan from my regular holidays. Pretty awesome right? I was quoted as being an entrepreneurial 'success' in online magazines, by my peers, industry and friends, and I often got asked what success meant to me in interviews with journalists and podcasters. Because I thought I had it, and had never really thought about it, I just used to answer that question with something vague like *'it's achieving whatever goals you have set for yourself'*.

But I've since realised that it's something very different indeed, and that everything I'd been subconsciously striving for for so long was all wrong.

During 2014, my company, MainTraining was primarily delivering training to the long term unemployed in remote communities throughout Australia, helping those with very minimal access to training and education to prepare for work within their local communities.

We were making a real and positive difference to people's lives and we had a business to be very proud of. I was living the entrepreneurs dream with all that I had and all that I was doing.

Then, at 10:35 on a Tuesday morning in March 2015, I received a phone call that changed everything.

Without warning and only 19 months in to a 5 year promise, the Federal Government, who funded our clients' terminated the budget.
No warning, no 'teach out' period, nothing. Just a complete and deadly lethal blow to my business, and hundreds of others like mine all over Australia.
One by one my customers called me to tell me that all work had to cease immediately.
My heart shattered into pieces as I thought of all the people we wouldn't be able to help anymore, at the thought of how on earth I was going to find wages for my 23 staff.

Slowly the enormity of my situation came to haunt me. We had paid bookings for venues, flights and accommodation in remote communities that had to be cancelled. The saddest part was that our programs were being so well received by our participants who were otherwise forgotten about due to their remoteness, and now we could no longer help them out.
As if that wasn't bad enough, tenders we'd spent months and months on securing, worth millions of dollars were suddenly pulled out from underneath us. The bright looking future was all of a sudden very dark and scary.

How would I tell my team that I'd failed them? How could I have allowed myself to put everything at risk by only having ONE income stream? This was in fact all my fault. I had built a beautiful one-legged stool and put all of my eggs on top of it; and it had toppled over into a terrifying mess.

Somehow, I managed to hold it together until my staff left for the day. When the last employee closed the office door behind them, I was deafened by the silence.
I walked around the office feeling like my life had ended, looking at the empty desks, normally buzzing with activity and the beautiful sounds of training developers singing to the latest pop songs.
I picked up one of the recent feedback forms posted back from the Mid-West agriculture and horticultural course.

'You've changed my life MainTraining' stared up at me - and now it all was gone.

I vomited in the waste paper bin beside my PA's desk and cried on my office floor for hours.

Now five months later, I have used this experience to dramatically change the way I do business and as an opportunity to reflect on my life as an entrepreneur and businesses woman, and because I choose to see my adversity as a lesson and an opportunity; I chose to create an awards ceremony instead of giving in to depression.

Down but definitely not out, I decided to put my energy into finding a way of celebrating, recognising and appraising other hardworking 'Edupreneurs' like me. To raise awareness of the level of effort and commitment that entrepreneurs who 'give' (instead of JUST 'hustle') put out there.
To thank these unsung and silent heroes for not only contributing to our economy, but also to the knowledge and skills of our population across industry sectors; for without learning and progression we are nothing - and if I didn't thank them, nobody would.

And so it was born. In less than 8 weeks, I single handedly pulled together, from nothing, The Edupreneur Awards.
I didn't have time for getting sponsors, but that wasn't going to put me off. I wiped away my tears of self-pity, pulled my sleeves up and got networking. In just 8 short weeks, I received entries from 100 award nominees, from more than 5 countries and the nominations site had over 60,000 views - without any advertising!
I now run the awards annually in many countries to continue to celebrate businesses that give back and to encourage more sharing of information and education. It's my dream to have celebrated and recognised 10,000 edupreneurs by 2025 in many countries.

This only came about because I recognised that in this adversity there was an opportunity. I recognised that I had not been dealt a bad hand, but had been given the opportunity to wear the Captain's hat to lead the way of a new era.

So what is success?

In entrepreneurship, I think it's impossible to pick any one achievement as a unique success. Every success comes from a string of interconnected actions, strategies and efforts - they also come out of the way we handle commonplace failure and setbacks.
I made over 7 figures in my first two years in a new business in a new country; attained over $3million in funding for training for my clients; instigated the vocational education of thousands of Australian workers, provided welfare to work education to the long term unemployed in remote Australian communities, planned the career pathways of hundreds of careers in the mining, construction and oil and gas industry in some of Australasia's biggest resources projects, written training that will educate endless students through Registered Training Organisations, a flying school, corporate businesses and even military personnel.
All of this and more in just 2 years, at 29 years old.
Whilst I am extremely proud of all of this, these 'results are no longer what I consider as my successes.

The achievement I am most proud of, the thing I define as my greatest success, is not any asset or moment of glory; but the fact that I've never given up.

Sticking it out, instead of crumbling during the many times of frustration, stress and pain is my success.
Striving forward when I felt lost and alone is my success.
Refusing to accept that I'd exhausted every option when it seemed no choices were left; and finding the humility to laugh at myself when i was taking it all too seriously are my successes.
Starting a business with absolutely no money (as most start-ups do), but also with no phone, no laptop, no home and no friends or contacts - was made even riskier and harder as I was the only income-earner at the time. To make it tougher, having just moved to Australia, I didn't even have a visa, let alone furniture or bedding. (I slept on a towel on the floor for my first three months in business - yet still brought in $250,000 from nothing). How? Because my greatest success is that I chose to not give up.

Maintaining resilience, hard work and strategically selected action-taking when you feel overwhelmed and 'up against it', is success.

Sticking it out when you've pulled endless thankless hours, haven't slept in weeks, and don't have a boss to give you a day off, a bonus or a grateful pat on the back, is the REAL success of all entrepreneurs.

The ones who face the fear, ride out the rough days, and still make great things happen that help other people are the successful ones.

Therefore, it's not what we attain in terms of tangible goods or status that determines our success, but actually the quality of the constant and never-ending choices we make. For every choice we make, determines the action we take, which determines how others see and treat us in response, which gives us our feedback about our level of effectiveness, which finally determines our outcome, or overall experience. I call this, 'The Efficacy Effect' which is shown below.

Model of The Efficacy Effect - Sarah Cordiner 2015

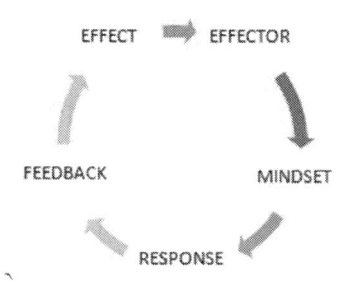

```
        EFFECT  ➡  EFFECTOR
       ↗                ↘
  FEEDBACK            MINDSET
       ↖                ↙
          RESPONSE
```

Understanding the Efficacy Effect will allow anyone who has a desire to influence their own life paths and experiences, to ultimately create success in their everyday life.

The 'Butterfly Effect', coined by Edward Lorenz in 1961 describes how a small change in one place, can result in a much bigger change later on; such as how a butterfly flapping its wings in one place can create a hurricane in another place under the right conditions. It is about how a seemingly trivial event can create an extremely different result than would have happened, if the minor event hadn't occurred. This is exactly how the Efficacy Effect works.

The tiniest actions and choices we make can alter our entire life paths.

Everything we have, or don't have, is influenced by our perceived ability, or inability to succeed in any given activity.

But the thing is, these perceptions are built by our collective past experiences, our environment, culture and social groups instead of a factual analysis of our real abilities; meaning many of us make major life choices and off-the-cuff decisions based on false interpretations, misled mindsets about our ability and even delusional concepts of our competence to achieve.

But here's the magic:
- the learned can be unlearned
- the truth can be discovered
- new habits and behaviours can be conditioned, and awareness can be raised.

If any single human did not have the ability to learn, to grow, or to achieve, she would not be able to articulate a language to tell you of her perceived inabilities or problems in the first place. Human beings have untapped potential, all it takes to release it, is a little bit of efficacy.

In my book 'The Eff Word', you will learn how to unleash a LOT of efficacy; in yourself, and in others.

Your level of efficacy, or belief in your ability to create success results; has exponential effects on your psychological and physical health and wellbeing, your achievements, and the entire course that your life will take. It bears significant influence on your academic performance, educational attainment, vocational pursuits and level of professional success.

Your level of efficacy determines the choices you make, the actions you do or do not commit, the kind of life you build for yourself, and how you react and adapt in challenging circumstances.

The most important thing to remember is that every experience begins with a choice, and that choice will determine your outcome.

At 17 years old, I was given the opportunity to learn a very, very powerful lesson about making choices for success. When a friend of mine was extremely sick with Chron's disease, the dreaded day came when I was called to go to my friend to say my last goodbye to him.
As I sat beside his bed, I was surprised to find him happy and optimistic – not what I expected to see from a dying man.

"Why are you so happy?" I asked him. He looked at me very seriously, saying, *"Sarah, I want you to remember one thing, and I want you to never, ever forget this."*

With his hand shaking hard, he picked up a glass of water and placed it on the hospital bed-table in front of him. *"Sarah, bad things will always happen to you. There are things in life you cannot control. Whether it's a mean, jealous person, a marriage break up, or a serious illness – stuff will happen, and this cup represents all of the unpleasant, unexpected and disappointing things in life."* With that, he slammed the glass hard onto the table with a bang, sloshing water out onto the table around it.

"Never forget that 100% of the time, you have two choices".

He pointed to the left hand side of his glass of water, and said *"Choice number 1 Sarah, is when undesired things happen, and you allow them stop you. You allow them to become the excuse and the barrier to everything you do. You choose to allow them to leave you stuck until, eventually, you die".*

He paused for a moment to catch his breath and stop his hand from shaking so furiously. Pointing now to the right hand side of his glass, he continued, *"Choice number 2 Sarah, is when undesired things happen, but you choose to see them as an opportunity. It's when you choose to ask yourself, 'What can I learn from this?' or 'How can good come from this?' With this as your mindset, you choose to allow yourself to walk victoriously to the other side of any adversity a better, wiser and stronger person than you were before it happened".*
He finished by holding the glass up and peering over it from the opposite side that was originally facing him and wore a grin on his face again.

It was a profound moment as I realised that no matter what happened to me, I was ALWAYS in control of what my experience and overall result would be. I remind myself of this every time things don't go to plan, whether it's forgetting something at the supermarket, or losing millions of dollars and my entire workforce; for this reminder gives me a sense of control that ignites my self-efficacy and ultimately what the result will be. It reminds me that all it takes to live a life of what I call 'an efficacious existence', is to make one of two choices.

But hang on, didn't I start this chapter by saying that I went 10 years into my life without understanding what success was? What went wrong? How was it that I failed to learn this powerful lesson from my dying friend?

When I was a kid, we'd have really fun weekends away in the caravan, or playing in the farmers fields, or going on a magical mystery tour with Dad. But every single Monday morning, he'd dejectedly puff *'Well, back to reality'* as he pulled on his work boots looking like he'd just been told he was going to die.
It would always make my mind ponder and my heart sink, having seen him for two days as my superhero, the fun guy, the 'maker of dreams', suddenly become so obviously low.

It also made me confused. Whenever he groaned the words *'back to reality'* on a Monday morning I couldn't help but question why the weekends were 'unreal', but the weekdays were - and especially why something 'real' was bad.

I recall asking when I was 10 years old *"Daddy, why don't you like going back to reality?"*. *"You wouldn't understand darling"* he murmured as he reluctantly closed the front door behind him.

But I did understand. Dad didn't like going to this 'reality' place every week, but I never saw aliens abducting him every Monday, or club-laden giants dragging him out the front door, or a police man tying up his hands and dragging him away, or the military dropping through the chimney to carry him off in a helicopter against his will. All I saw was Dad *voluntarily* putting his boots on, and choosing to walk out of the door to a place he didn't want to go.

Why didn't he just stop going? Why didn't he go somewhere else instead? This reality place sounded ugly and stupid. But I thought Dad was even more stupid for going there every single day when he hated it so much.

When we're a kid, we see life very simply. We only spend our time doing things we enjoy doing, things that we find fun, enjoyable, entertaining and pleasurable. But as we get older, happiness and pleasure becomes secondary to what we think we 'should' be doing; to what society and the people around us expect us to be doing. Until eventually we find ourselves in jobs we hate, doing things day in and day out that make us categorically miserable. And the worst part is, we forget we have a choice about it.

I promised myself when I was 10 years old, that I would never go to this 'reality' place.

But just like most of the other 6 billion people on earth, I did. Adulthood brings an onset of demands, and the suffocation of freedom. We can find ourselves feeling unexplainably dissatisfied with life, even if it looks 'perfect' from the outside. We find ourselves stuck, but don't know why or how to become 'unstuck'.

We can feel like our life, responsibilities and circumstances are in complete control of us, like we cannot possibly change anything because we HAVE to do what we have to do. Or, we think we're in control because we're doing everything we're supposed to be doing, but in fact, we are actually enabling the existence of a reality that we absolutely do NOT want.

I saw my Dad as the heroic 'maker of dreams' at the weekends, and I think he saw his weekend self that way too. But like most of us, he magically forgot he had this super power of choice every Monday morning and went back to following the script to a play he didn't even like.

The script we play out IS our reality, regardless of what day it is. Unless you are being dragged out of your beds every morning by club-laden giants, the SAS lassoing you up your chimney, or alien abductions, you must see that you have chosen to live this reality.
All my dad had to do was change the reality by making a different choice or taking a different action.

What reality would *you* rather be in?

18 years after deciding my Dad was stupid for choosing to accept a reality he hated, I woke up one Monday morning absolutely dreading the day ahead of me. I hated my job, I hated my boss, I hated everyone I worked with, and I'm pretty sure they hated me even more. I couldn't leave, I was the only income earner at the time, I didn't yet have a visa as I'd just moved to a new country and ironically considered myself 'lucky' to have this job, even though it made me want to boil my head in acid.
On this Monday morning, I considered inventing an illness, faking my own death, or hoping it was a public holiday I'd forgotten about. No such luck, I'm too proud to fake sickies – and I was on a casual contract so wouldn't have got paid the money we desperately needed anyway. I HAD to go in and play out my duties. I reluctantly stuffed on my uncomfortable shoes, and as I dragged myself out of the front door exhaled a huge, defeated puff of misery with the words *'huuuffff, back to reality'*.

I stopped dead on my doorstep in complete and utter shock. My heart sank. I saw myself 10 years old, peering saddened through the window at my daddy driving off to the 'reality' he hated and me thinking he was stupid for doing so. Yet here I was, breaking my own promise to myself and doing it too; failing to learn the most important life lesson my dad inadvertently had taught me.

I remembered I had a choice as my 10 year old self appeared in front of me asking *'Why don't we go somewhere else instead?'* I did go to work that morning; to hand in my resignation. The next day I started on recreating for myself what I call, a life of 'efficacious existence'. A life of desired results, a life of my own desired reality. A life of uncovering my *own* definition of 'success'. If you don't know what that is for you yet, first of all just identify what it's NOT.

In my book 'The Eff Word' and on my Facebook page 'Sarah Cordiner', I share with readers how you can fire up your super power of being an 'efficacy effector' for yourself. So now when I think about what success is, I think more about what it's not. For success, in my eyes, is anything but giving up or giving in to your circumstances when faced with undesirable and challenging circumstances. If my story can tell you anything, I hope it tells you this:

You are in control of everything in your life, *not* the adversities and challenges which you may be facing. You are in control of your life, your reality, your Monday morning, your job, your problems. Life is *your* bitch because you can choose how to respond to your challenges, and what results you get. there is no magical epiphany, there is no 'good luck and bad luck'; there is only choice and action.

Choosing the right ones is what uncovers success.

To your success.

Sarah

About the Author

Sarah Cordiner is an author, qualified trainer, & global thought leader in 'Edupreneurship', 'Edu-marketing', Entrepreneurship, Efficacy and Education.

She is a specialist in training development and curriculum design, as well as trainer of trainers in adult learning.

She is the CEO of MainTraining; Winner of the 'Influential 100 Awards 2015'; Founder of 'The Edupreneur Awards', Founder of Edupreneur Magazine,

Ambassador and peer advisor for 'TribeLearn' and The Institute For Professional Speakers and is a Nominee of The Telstra Business Women's Awards 2015.

Sarah's Keynote & Expert Topics:

- Education
- Teaching & Learning Practices; The Hidden Curriculum; and Curriculum/Instructional Design and Development

- Entrepreneurship
- What entrepreneurs and businesses in any industry can learn about growing business by using the platform of education instead of sales; and how to write profitable learning products and programs as a lead/income generation tool

- Workforce Planning & Development
- How corporates can maximise their productivity and profitability by effectively utilising their workforce skills and capabilities

- Students Transitioning From Education To Employment
- What's next and what do employers really want? What to do after your degree.

- Overcoming Adversity
- How actively creating adversity as well as effectively coping with it is the key to success in life and business

Sarah's work has enabled the education of thousands of workers; helped welfare dependents in remote Australian communities (and throughout the UK) progress to employment, initiated the movement of 'Edupreneurship' and assisted other training providers to deliver excellent training.

"I have dedicated my life to providing engaging and transformative education to the world. I have designed, written and delivered curriculum to prisons, schools, universities, businesses, Government and charities internationally; as well as helped other training providers and entrepreneurs through edupreneurship, teacher-training and curriculum/instructional design".

With a PGCE, a BA (Hons) Degree in Education and 10 years in business, Sarah knows a thing or two about combining business with education to create a potent elixir of growth for entrepreneur and audience alike.

Follow Sarah: https://www.facebook.com/efficacyeffect

It Takes a Long Time to Become an Overnight Success

Talking about success as an adult is a lot like talking about sex in high school— no one knows exactly what it is or how to get it, but everyone wants to have it. Time and time again, we are told that success takes different forms depending on the person and their values. I don't disagree that success can be viewed from multiple vantage points; however, the path to achieving success is the same no matter which area of your life you're trying to achieve it.

Before I begin introducing you to my personal philosophies on success, I would like to introduce you to the person behind them: yours truly. My name is Alexandra Tonks and I am a co-founder at ZomeChat, a San Francisco-based tech company. As much as I would love to go into my personal story of my rise to success (because who doesn't love talking about themselves?), I really don't think that would be very beneficial to you. When most people tell their "success story" of how they got to where they are, it sounds great, but it isn't *real*. The story they tell is usually a compilation of the highlights of their journey, but it isn't their *story*. They may include a failure or two for dramatic effect, but they don't include the times when they didn't do anything, the times when just random luck blew opportunity their way, or the times when they did everything wrong, but somehow it ended up working out. The most important error that these stories make is not even that they leave out these "times," but that they leave out the entire element of time. Every one of the stories I read about "rags to riches," never includes time as being much of a factor at all. It's as if people from Eastern Europe would just arrive in America and instantly become rich based purely on work ethic from the old country. How ridiculous would that be? We know it's too crazy to believe it, but a part of us does. We think about how it was so easy for someone else, but for us, it's a never-ending struggle. We complain about "why can't life be easier for us?" My assumption is, that no one has it that easy (even the guy you're pointing at, wishing you had his life). In fact, the more I talk to other CEOs, I realize that everyone is just as lost as I am.

People say that entrepreneurs walk a path that has never been walked before—I couldn't disagree more. There is a path for entrepreneurs to follow, but the fact that it's a path less followed, automatically makes it more difficult. In addition, the path seems to disappear due to the fact that so many people get off track before they've ever reached their destination. Being a successful entrepreneur seems like an insurmountable task, but it's not—in fact, nothing is. In the rest of this chapter, I will argue that success, in any area of life, is attributed to a combination of definiteness, patience, and consistency.

The first step to actualizing your success is to have definiteness about what you want to accomplish. Figuring out what you want is most certainly the first step to getting it. Write down your immediate and long-term goals, but also your KPIs. In business, KPI stands for: Key Performance Indicators, they can range anywhere from downloads to sales, or even to employee's job satisfaction. In your personal life, KPIs can take the form of how much money you make each month, how much sleep you're getting, how often you workout, etc. To exemplify the meaning of KPI and the purpose of exactness, I will set the stage for a little group bonding activity.

Let's look at one of my favorite team-bonding activities. In the activity, one person is blindfolded and the rest of the group has to lead this person, from afar, to a certain destination by yelling out how close "hot" or how far "cold" the person is from getting to end point. For our purposes, let's say that they're on a golf course. The precursor for this activity to work is that the destination has to be established and agreed upon by both the group and the blindfolded person beforehand. In the case of the golf course, we may set the destination to be the flagpole. Think about this in your life or organization: Have you and your team/family established where you're going? If not, maybe it's best to figure that out before you have a blindfolded zombie on the loose.

Equally as important, the team must work together to get the sightless member to their target. The blindfolded person has to be able to hear one unanimous voice as opposed to the voice of twenty individuals. Back to thinking about your life: does your organization have one clear voice that represents the values and direction of where you're going? You should probably think about the difference in power between a smooth long boat horn and the noise of thirty seagulls yelping out different variations of, "Mine!"

For the group to succeed in this activity, they need to be constantly checking in with the blindfolded person to see how he or she is doing on the journey to the flagpole. This is where you'll find your key performance indicators. If we're reflecting on our personal life, then check in with yourself and your family. If it's in your business, then check in with your employees and the status of your profits. You need to know when you're cold versus hot to be able to stay on your path to success. You really need to make sure you're listening to when these key performance indicators start communicating with you. Put yourself in the shoes of the person with the blindfold: how far off are you from the track to your goal? Are you listening to others who are telling you how far off you are? Being successful seems like a daunting task, but it's really nothing more than leading a blind person down a golf course. Just kidding...well, sort of.

We now understand the importance of knowing where we're going. No one wants to be the zombie on the golf course or the group indefinitely yelling directions at him or her. Now, the next step is to make a commitment to actually get there. Warning: it may take a long time to get to where you want to be; accept it and keep going. Looking back to the example, imagine how absolutely frustrating it would be to struggle listening to "hot" and "cold" over and over again? How tempted would you be to just take the blindfold off? This is when faith and determination result in patience. Yes, you will get frustrated, but if you give up, then you will never get where you want to go. Whatever you do, do not take off that blindfold. If you do, you will have to start all over and be faced with all of the same obstacles over and over again. This is exactly what happens in companies. When the going gets rough in a startup, the leaders of the company sometimes choose to abandon it for the next "million-dollar idea" they have. Let me tell you a secret: it's not the idea that's the problem. Once you leave a startup to start another one, you are faced with beginning the process all over again. Some people make excuses for themselves and say that they like the clean slate—I'm not one of those people and you shouldn't be either. Of course, you may realize that the flagpole you thought you were on the path to turned out to be a sand dune and you need to either start over or change directions, but you would only be able to realize that if you stayed on the path long enough.

Well you might be wondering: how long does it take to become successful? Well according to Malcolm Gladwell's book, <u>Outliers</u>, it takes about 10,000 hours to be an expert at anything. That's a lot of hours. To put that into perspective, a rough estimate of a full-time college student's work load (about 45 hours a week) leads us to conclude that by graduation they would've spent 5,760 hours in school or on schoolwork. That only meets half the requirement. I suppose I understand why it makes sense that education is not enough these days. College graduates need about another 5,000 hours of work before they can consider themselves really knowledgeable in any certain field.

Take the time to really consider how much time you've put into something before you write it off as not being in the cards. Also, as a little piece of advice, if you don't want to wait for exactly 10,000 hours to go by before you're really good at something, then choose something you're already good at. When I was much younger, I had a burning desire to become a professional DJ. However, after I took a few lessons—yes, I took DJ lessons—I realized that I couldn't hear the difference between the music in my headphones and the music playing through the loud speakers. I couldn't blend songs together (the whole purpose of a DJ) because I couldn't tell which music was faster or slower than the other. I could have spent 10,000 hours training my ears to be able to tell the difference and I could have become a great DJ, but I was a highly impatient person at that time in my life and I decided to stick with a strategy that I already had a strong background in: problem solving.

So, at this point you know that it's going to take a long time to become successful. You've come to grips with it, maybe you've even bought yourself a comfy chair to sit back in and wait until enough time has passed. Life is so easy, right? (If anything is *that* easy, run, don't walk, quickly away!) The catch is that you actually have to do something, but the secret is: (wait for it) it doesn't have to be much. Shocking? I know, but hear me out. Imagine that each day, you take a small Lego block and stick it on to another one.

Your goal is to build a house (definiteness). If each day you add one Lego onto the Lego you placed down the day before, by the time you've reached 100 days, you'll have a pretty substantial house (patience and consistency). You might be thinking to yourself that you could build that house in one day, one hundred days is absurd to wait. You're right, you probably could build it in one day, but you won't. You'll most likely put it off and make excuses for yourself everyday until you've hit the hundred-day mark. You tell yourself that you could build that house any day of the week, so you put it off and let other things get in the way of your goal getting completed. The really amazing thing about understanding human nature is getting around it.

By getting yourself to put down one Lego a day, you get rid of your ability to make excuses for yourself. That is the power of consistency my friend. Our actions that we do every day, little by little, add up until we reach our desired effect. Jeff Olsen, in his book, <u>The Slight Edge</u>, discusses the power of simple daily activities along with the compounding effect of time. That's really all it is. A day goes by and you didn't add a Lego, your house isn't going to break down, but it's also not going to get any bigger. However, consistency allows us to use time as a multiplier of our energy in the most efficient way possible. We only need to put down one Lego a day and that's really the only amount we should do. You're going to have to break the expectations you have with yourself and with others that success happens overnight. I can honestly tell you that I've stayed up many a night hoping that my work will bring grand success the next day and to my dismay it doesn't. Only through definiteness, patience, and consistency will we ever be able to achieve "overnight success"—but use these tools and the world is yours.

Alexandra Tonks

About the author

Alexandra Tonks is a graduating senior at the University of California, Berkeley. She has started two companies in her time there and is continuing to grow her second, ZomeChat. ZomeChat is a social, mobile app that connects members and visitors of a community through location-based chat-rooms and newsfeeds. She prides her app on giving people the power to feel like a local no matter where they are and making the world feel even smaller. Alexandra is a dedicated entrepreneur, student, and daughter.

Vitality and Vibration - How to Manage Your Energy to Create The Life You Want!

Define *Vibrational Frequency:* Vibrational frequency is defined as the rate at which the atoms and sub-particles of a being or object vibrate (Oxford Dictionary)

Define *Vitality*: The state of being strong and active; energy or the power giving continuance of life, present in all living things (Oxford Dictionary).

Before we get into creating the life you want, let's all get onto the same page here, so to speak. We don't want to be discussing vitality and energy management without a basic understanding of what it is and how it applies to you.

Let's go back and start with a little high school physics.

I know - I know. I didn't exactly excel or love it either however I assure you that *some* of what you learned will apply here.

You'll be grateful you didn't fall asleep during every science lesson in high school - promise!

Let's break it down here - really simply - so we're working from the same understanding…

   a. Inside you, there a billions of cells *[you already know that, right?]*
   b. Inside each of these cells are myriad cool things *[which we will go into in more detail later]* however at the most basic level, cells are made up of clusters of millions of *atoms*.
   c. An atom itself is made up of three tiny kinds of particles called *subatomic particles*: protons, neutrons, and electrons.

d. The protons and the neutrons make up the center of the atom called the *nucleus* and the electrons fly around above the nucleus in a small cloud.
e. These subatomic particles also have huge amounts of space between them. That space is often referred to as a vacuum because it is nothing - not air, not matter - it is nothing. In that nothing though is pure energy. It is vibrating energy - moving - all the time.

The atom bomb was developed by way of using this energy - from splitting 'open' an atom - and redirecting it. You know the result of that - huge power, huge explosions - the greatest release of energy known to man.

So...

Why does any of that matter?

On the most basic level, under your skin, organs, skeleton; under the cells, atoms and sub-atomic particles you are nothing more than energy. Pure and simple - vibrating energy. You are loads and loads and loads of vibrating energy.

Given that you are energy - vibrating - we can apply what is called a "frequency" of vibration. The frequency of vibration is the level at which the energy is vibrating, its the number of WAVES of vibration (see image).

Everything is vibration - thought, matter, things, feelings, sound, water. It's all vibration and it's all at various frequencies. The frequency - or measured number of waves - is what determines that a water wave stays as seen as a wave of water or that a sound wave is heard as sound, and not the other way around.

The frequency of vibration is the number given to a scale that maps the level of vibration. For example, pitch in music or tone in speaking is a change in the vibrational frequency - or number of waves - and is interpreted differently by the ear bones responding to the frequency of vibration, or number of waves. Get it?

Here is a great infographic to explain it quickly and simply:

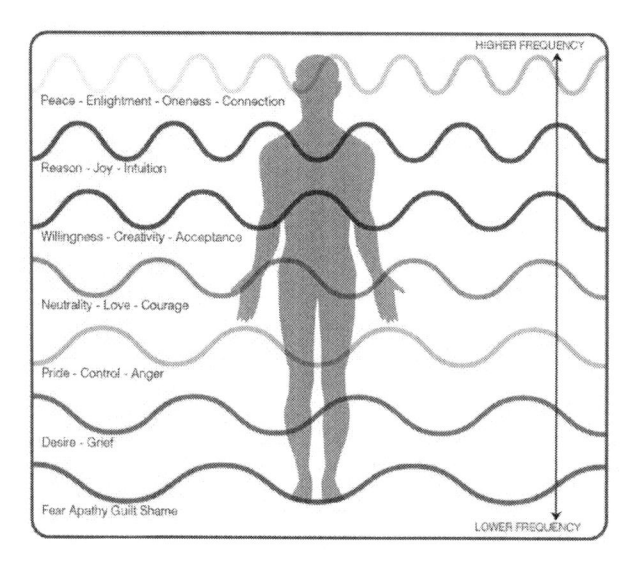

[Infographic showing a human silhouette with wave frequencies labeled from higher to lower frequency: Peace - Enlightment - Oneness - Connection; Reason - Joy - Intuition; Willingness - Creativity - Acceptance; Neutrality - Love - Courage; Pride - Control - Anger; Desire - Grief; Fear Apathy Guilt Shame]

Now we loop all the back to the first definition of the chapter:

Vibrational Frequency: Vibrational frequency is defined as the *rate at which the atoms and sub-particles of a being or object vibrate.*

Why is vitality even remotely important to creating the life that you want?

Think about it like this... have you ever known someone who has an amazing life?

The kind of life that makes you stop and wonder what they're doing differently, why they're so blessed and why God favours them above everyone else?

They have wonderful relationships with their family and friends, they are wealthy, they are physically healthy and strong, they are joyous and have an infectious energy that stops you dead in your tracks.

These people have rich, full lives. They are also full of vitality - exuberance, energy, zeal, passion and enthusiasm. They may live life to the fullest - in that they may love to celebrate like the best of us - however they manage their energy and vitality well because their life demands it.

They live lives of continuous *joy*.

Think about the most successful people on the planet that for whom energy is a pivotal part of who they are and what they do. Think of people who stand out as having constantly re-created themselves, having constantly achieved more and More and MORE and who live lives earmarked not so much by their achievements but their longevity and joyful attitudes.

People like…

- Bob Proctor
- Richard Branson
- Nelson Mandela

Could these people been even half as successful as they have been had they not had extraordinary vitality, lived with extraordinary joy? There is no way!

These people re-create themselves and succeed again and again and again because they manage their energy with careful precision. Their diet, their exercise regime, their home life - it's all carefully planned, thought through and executed to ensure maximum energy, maximum vitality, maximum joy is the result.

In short, they lived *joyful* lives - not just successful ones - that they created *on purpose*.

Here is another graphic that explains this concept quickly and simply:

OMEGA

700+	Enlightenment	
600	Peace	
540	Joy	
500	Love	
400	Reason	
350	Acceptance	▶ Oneness / Opening / Higher Consciousness
310	Willingness	
250	Neutrality	
200	Courage	
175	Pride	
150	Anger	
125	Desire	
100	Fear	▶ Disconnected / Closing / Survival Consciousness
75	Grief	
50	Apathy	
30	Guilt	
20	Shame	

ULTIMATE CONSCIOUSNESS

ALPHA POINT

Notice how as you move up the scale of human emotion - from negative feelings to positive feelings - the waves of thought as noted in the other graphic move closer together. The higher the frequency of emotion - the better the feelings you feel - the closer the waves and therefore the more intense is the signal you are emitting.

Vitality - joyful energy - is the single most important thing you can do for yourself if you want to create a life you love. Without joy - without vitality - you may achieve some temporary greatness, however you will not sustain it.

The last 5 centuries - and indeed beyond - are littered with the achievements of many great people. These great people definitely achieved certain levels of success however it was not sustained. These achievers often succumbed to tragic ends.

Things like terminal illness, bankruptcy, suicide and poverty punctuate the ends of the lives of many great men and women in times gone by.

Yes, there were the rich or infamous - in one sense - but they lacked essential vitality, joyful energy. Their lives lacked the higher vibrations of thought and emotion.

To put it simply, there was a lack of sustainable sources of joy. This, it appears, was their undoing.

People like...

- Walt Disney
- Michael Jackson
- Elvis Presley
- Vincent Van Gough
- Ernest Hemingway

These amazing people achieved levels of success that most only dream of, yet their lives are characterised by a serious lack of vitality - lack of joyful energy - which eventually became their own demise.

You can study their downfalls and you will see the signs that their vitality - joyful energy - was not at the level it needed to be to sustain their success. There was substance abuse, violence, abuse, mental and physical illness, poverty, isolation and more.

These amazingly talented people certainly changed the world however the changes they created may also have become the death of them.

Why?

Because the lives they were attempting to create - the changes they were making in the world - vibrated at very high frequencies. This is why these people are so memorable! Their *legacies* are an incredibly high frequency of vibration. They themselves however may not have been able to match the frequency at which their achievements were vibrating.

In essence, their lives became 'larger' than themselves. This is certainly the case where there was longstanding illness, poverty, crime or suicide.

Alternatively they may have decided on an unconscious - or superconscious level - that they had done what they had set out to do in this life, in this world and it was time for them to return to their pure state of being. A state of unlimited vibrational frequency where there density of the vibration of this world was no longer weighing them down.

This could be the case with those that left suddenly - those that 'went out on a high' - so to speak.

It all depends on how you look at it and how their lives manifested whilst they were still here with us. It is indeed worth studying the very successful and their downfall. It is even more worthwhile making a study of the truly successful who lived lives of joy, success, enthusiasm *and* achievement.

Many great lessons can be learned by standing on the shoulders of the men who have gone before you.   As the saying goes "To be successful you need to study the successful".

Why Does Vitality Matter?

The answer to this question, really, is pure logic.

Let me ask you this question: How can you expect to lead a HUGE life - of riches, fame, health and all that you desire - with the frequency of vibration - the energy level - of a poor person who doesn't look after themselves?

Newton's Third Law of Motion (often referred to as the First Law of Physics which is not quite correct) states that for every action there is an equal and opposite RE-action.

Meaning that it stands to reason that if you want a larger than life type of life, YOU yourself must be larger than life. You must feel the larger than life feelings - joy, peace, love. You must immerse yourself in these feelings as often as you can so that the balance of your emotions as you go about your daily life is tipped in the favour of higher frequencies; meaning you need to feel better more often than you feel worse. You can not sustain a "larger than life" type of life in any other way.

Vitality is essential to life - it's your life force. You simply can not create the life of your dreams until you have the vitality - the joyful energy levels - to match. You may be able to get a taste of that life here and there; you may even sustain your dream life for a year or two - maybe even ten years - but eventually you will crash and burn.

Why?

Because you lacked the essential energy to sustain such a vital life. Your life became bigger than you; was more vital than you; vibrating higher than you are - and it burned you out.

Think about it this way... look back at the two graphics pictured. Your life's goals and dreams and desires are all vibrating in the TOP HALF of the spectrum. If you feel worse more often than you feel better then you yourself are vibrating LOWER than the goals you have. How can you hope to attract what you want if you're not sending out the right signals? If you're sending out signals - by feeling certain ways - of fear, dread, anxiety, regret, worry etc then you will simply attract more things to fear, to regret and so on.

To create the life you love, you MUST concentrate your thoughts on finding sustainable sources of joy. In fact this is one of the single most important things you can do - far more important than taking constant action from a place of frustration, lack or fear.

When things are not going how to I want them to go in my life or in my business, I will contact my team and say "I am going offline to do the hippie thing". They laugh at me - thinking it's all very amusing "hippie" fluffy type stuff - however when I come back online there has usually been a deposit of a large amount of money, or the acquisition of a major client or some other apparently miraculous windfall.

My team know - despite their snickering - the my going offline to do "the hippie thing" is me taking time out to step away and go into a place of joy. If I don't do that then things quickly descend and it's a much tougher job to right the situation.

For example - I remember a day not so long ago. It was Mercury Retrograde - which usually means you are going to be slowed down and forced to go back over old ground particularly where communication, business, travel and the like are concerned. It can be a very frustrating time for a control freak like I used to be.

I was trying to meet a deadline that was looming large. My systems kept locking up or freezing, the computer was freezing up, the printer kept failing... nothing worked!

I ended up trying to force the issue - thinking of this looming deadline, hating to let anyone down - and I paid the price.

After an hour of trying to get my systems working and my computer back online I shouted in sheer exasperated frustration and slammed the laptop shut. When I opened it again a few minutes later what should be waiting for me?

A black screen. Not even the "Blue Screen of Death". No. Just black. Nothing else.

The hard drive had crashed. Completely. I lost everything on it.

I knew then that I had no other choice - and I should have seen it sooner - but to step back and leave it all.

I had forced, pushed, and tried to hide from the Laws of Nature by thinking I could do it all from a space of frustration, lethargy, lack and agitation.

I couldn't. The Laws of Nature and indeed Nature Herself knew better and I got a lesson. An expensive one.

Now, when I am feeling like that I simply stop.

I have learned - through observing myself repeating the same scenario over and over numerous times - that if I keep pushing - forcing - from a space of negative emotion, from a place of low vitality that I will indeed screw things up - and fast.

- I have lost clients that were a sure thing coming from a place of low energy, low vibration, low vitality.
- I have had electronics shut down, freeze up and break down because I was in a space of low vibration, low vitality.
- I have had my children throw the most amazing, intense and outrageous tantrums over (so it appeared) absolutely nothing - because I was in a space of low energy, low vitality.

In all these situations, I was not joyous.

I was mightily peeved!

And I was forcing an outcome - that I was far too attached too - from a space of very intense low frequency. Within no time at all, that intensity of emotion screws up my day and anything I touch turns to muck.

Instead of having the Midas Touch - which is what you have when you vibrate at a higher frequency; one of joyful energy - I have what I refer to as the "Shitas Touch". A little crass I know however you get the point I am trying to make.

My team laugh about it but they do so knowingly. They too have seen what happens when I force an outcome from a low frequency of vibration. They often tell me to "take a timeout" or "clock off" if I am not having a good day. I tell them the same thing!

I don't want my team working at something when they are tired, frustrated, angry or over it! Whatever they're working on will be tainted with that energy and trust me - nothing good comes from that space, that place of negative emotion.

I have sent my team home early numerous times - ordered them to have a glass of wine and dance to their favourite music or a hot bath or to go out somewhere nice for a great meal - so they can shift their energy and find what we call "Their Happy Place".

When they have done that, then they are ready to come back to work. That is the place where great things ensue!

Managing your vitality - your level of frequency of vibration or your joyful energy - is an absolutely vital part of creating the life you want.

Those people in your life that have incredible joy, enthusiasm and who live lives of wonderment are working within the Laws of Nature. They have accepted them and they use them to their own advantage. They know that by feeling good they will attract the good things out of life. Pure and simple.

It might sound like a very fluffy and "hippie" concept when it's anything but. Every thought has a frequency that can be measured. Every emotion has a frequency that can be measured. Quantum Physics is the study of this phenomenon of energy. Albert Einstein was a genius when it came to this information.

What do you think $E = MC^2$ was mostly about?! Energy!

How Do You Increase Vitality?

Vibrating at higher frequencies for long periods of time can be hard - if you're not used to it. If you've been vibrating in a lower frequency - feeling stressed, anxious, depressed, worried, fearful or full of regrets - then this will be a big change for you. It will take an equal amount - if not more - focus of energy to change the frequency of your vibration, or how you feel.

Raising your vibration - feeling joyful energy and enthusiasm - is something you need to support yourself into, something you need to plan for. There are those that can get up out of bed and feel joyful but guess what... they went through the process of raising their vibration consciously and consistently first - applying effort, focus and will power. Now it is a habit for them. I assure you that it wasn't always that way.

The purest form of joy is found in a baby - a laughing baby.

As we age, we start to lose touch with that state. We become immersed in the world around us - a world of stress, anxiety, debt, depression, war and the like - and we start to become 'infected' - for want of a better word - by these lower vibrations and these negative feelings.

So how do we shake that off? How do we increase our vitality?

The single most important thing you can do to increase your vitality is to focus ONLY on feeling good.

In fact, that is the only thing you need to do.

Now, that all sounds a bit too simplistic for some so let's break it down into some actionable steps you can take.

The 5 Step Program For Increasing Vitality

1. **Make a List**

    Write out a list of things that make you feel good.

    It could be music you love, a place you like to visit, food you enjoy, people who elevate your spirits, meditation, prayer, dancing, singing, cooking, gardening, knitting, petting your dog or cat... anything that leaves you feel good /positive / inspired / motivated / enthusiastic / joyful / content / peaceful needs to go on this list.

2. **Put Yourself into a State of Joy**

    Find time - make time to deliberately and consciously put yourself into a state of joy.

    Choose something from the list and do it for at least 15 minutes a day - longer if you can. If you love to dance and sing, then dance and sing to your favourite music every day! If you love to bake, then bake (and give it all away if you can't eat it all!) Whatever makes you feel good - do it! Give yourself permission to feel good - every. single. day.

    No exceptions.

3. **Focus On The Positives.**

    When something happens in your day that does not leave you feeling good, do not focus your attention upon it. Deliberately think thoughts to remove your attention from it and onto something else. One way to do that is to ask positive leading questions of yourself, in your mind. Questions like:

    - How can I turn this around?
    - What is great about this?

- What can I learn from this?
- How can I have done that differently?

These questions will force your mind to tune into a more positive vibrational frequency. Once you start on this path - keep going! Keep asking positive leading questions, keep focused on the positives that lay in the situation. They are always there - sometimes you might have to dig a bit deeper.

4. **There Is ALWAYS A Solution!**

   I remember speaking to one of my team recently when we were going through a bit of sticky situation with the company. It had been a little bit of a tyrade of challenges and we were both feeling a bit low energy. She said to me "How can you be so positive all the time?! I don't know how you do it!"

   My response was this:

   I wasn't always so positive. In fact, there was a time in my life when I was drowning - literally - in negative energy. I was suicidally depressed for my entire teenage life and so heavily medicated that I barely remember any of it.

   What working through that - and many other life challenges of which I have had my share - has taught me is that there is always Always ALWAYS a solution to ANY challenge we face. We may not see it - we may not want it - that doesn't mean it's not there.

   Being a graduate from the School of Hard Knocks, and a Professor at the University of Life (ha!) has taught me two things - resourcefulness and resilience. If you can just keep going and keep asking the questions above "How do I turn this around? How can I make this better?" you will find the answers. Always.

Why? Because you're emitting the vibrational frequency of finding answers!

By using the word "challenge" instead of problem, you are sending the signal to your subconscious mind and to the Universe that this is something to be overcome. Using the word "problem" sends the signal of being beaten, downtrodden, failing and the like. This is not the vibrational frequency of solutions - this is the frequency of the exact opposite!

There IS always a solution - to any challenge we face at any time we face it. We just have to shift our vibrational frequency - the way we are feeling about the challenge - to one of seeking solutions, of overcoming, of turning the situation around for the better. Once we find that space, that feeling, and maintain that vibration through seeking joy and higher frequency feelings solutions will come.

It is Law.

5. **Maintenance. Maintenance. Maintenance.**

   You can not follow this 5 Step Program for a week and expect to change your life.

   Yes, there will be *some* effect however it will be short lived - just like your efforts were.

   This 5 Step Program is all about consistency and persistence. Living a life that you love is all about consistency and persistence. Success in business is all about consistency and persistence. Success in athletics is all about consistency and persistence. Success in academia is all about consistency and persistence.

Are we seeing a pattern developing here?

Success in life - in any area - is all about consistency and persistence.

That includes success in feeling good.

If you want to feel joyful - to increase your frequency of vibration - then you have to practice doing so. Every day.

You have to consistently place yourself into a feeling of joy - by doing things that make you feel joyful. Every day.

But What About Goal Setting and Visualising?

Do not get me wrong - goal setting is a vital part of success and creating the life you love. Creating success, creating a life you love can be summed up beautifully in this metaphor: an archer, aiming an arrow at a target.

Without goals and your list of desires written down - in present tense - then you are an archer who is not aiming his arrow at anything. Will you hit the target? Unlikely.

After you have written your goals though - then what?

This is where the *5 Step Program to Increasing Vitality* above really comes into its powerful own.

Instead of focusing all your time on visualising your goals when you're in a bad mood or when you're feeling tired, do it once when you feel REALLY good and then leave it.

Let it go out to the Universe and let it do its thing.

After that simply focus your energy on remaining joyful.

That is when you will allow whatever you want to create to come to you - because your vibration will be up high where your goals are desires are vibrating. You must bring your own personal frequency of vibration up into alignment - into resonance - with the vibration of that which you want to create in your life.

Creating The Life You Love - Exercise

1. Go somewhere where you will not be disturbed. Allow 15 minutes.
2. Put yourself into a state of joy. Hold it for 10 minutes or so.
3. Once you are feeling joyful, close your eyes
4. Visualise your goals - your life - the way you want it to be.
5. Come out of the exercise and release it. Go about your day

That's it!

You do not need to spend hours pouring over a piece of paper with your Life's Vision written on it, trying to hold the picture in your mind. Yes, that is a good start however it's much faster and more effective to utilise your energy to do the work for you.

Visualise your goals - yes.
Use your energy to power the vision.

Your mind can not tell the difference between something real and imagined.

The Universe will act on the signals you emit - the frequency of vibration you maintain in yourself.

So, simply put - find ways to feel good, feel good, then visualise and release.

Its a very simple, very powerful process. The key to its success - and indeed yours as we covered earlier - is consistency and persistence.

In Summary...

To sum up everything, let me put it very simply for you.

You can not achieve wealth if you feel poor.
You can not achieve health if you feel sick.
You can not achieve vitality if you feel tired.

And so on and so on...

The vibrational frequencies of wealth, health and vitality are *high* frequencies. They vibrate on the top end of the scale.

The feelings of being poor, sick and tired are not high vibrational frequencies, they are extremely low. They operate in the lowest part of the vibrational scale. You can not - will not - attract wealth, health and happiness by feeling poor, sick and tired.

So stop it! Stop it right now!

In fact, do it right this minute! Go outside - take a deep breath, open your arms wide and look up to the sky. Breathe deeply and release the tension. Now smile. Seriously! Smile big and broad and wide and stupid! No one is looking!

Do you feel better? Did you notice a shift in your energy? Yes? Good. Go with that. Now what else can you do - right now - to feel even better again? Go and do it! Put this book down, and go and do something that makes you feel really really good. Right now!

If you feel crap, you will attract just that - crap. It is the Laws of Nature.

You can not fight them or change them. So stop trying.

To create the life you love, you can do all the goal setting and visualising and action taking in the world. That's a great start. Without feeling good -

without managing your energy and frequency of vibration - your results will be slow in coming and will take great expenditure of effort.

Wouldn't you much rather tap into the power of unlimited energy and have that do the work for you? It can you know - and it will! You just have to focus on feeling good.

Shift your focus from action Action ACTION towards your goals to one of joy Joy JOY and you will see amazing things start to happen in your life.

I promise.

Louisa Forrest

About the author

Louisa is a single work at home mother of two children and is the founder and CEO of The Lavenderia Group. The Lavenderia Group encompasses 5 brands all geared towards creating sustainable solutions for families and businesses and creating positive impactful change to the planet as a whole.

A serial entrepreneur from a young age, her career includes over a decade of business development and sales, marketing, strategic planning, outsourcing strategy, events management and public speaking.

Louisa is a passionate eco-warrior, and is also working on a Bachelor of Complementary Health Sciences whilst raising her two children and a few chickens in her home in the Blue Mountains of Australia.

Re:Cognition Health and Success

Starting a business from scratch requires passion, energy, self-belief, drive and determination. Making a business successful requires all of this and much, much more. There are lots of mine fields and success, even with hard work, is not a forgone conclusion!

I started Re:Cognition Health with my business partner Tom Dent in 2011 with a laptop, lots of lattes and a vision to create better pathways for assessment, diagnosis and treatment for individuals presenting with symptoms of dementia and cognitive decline.

We set out to bring together the best doctors to offer a joined up approach to patient treatment and care, all available in one place. After 12 years working as a Neuroradiologist, I witnessed a very disjointed service and found it frustrating to watch individuals with early signs of dementia being left in the system, without really efficient treatment plans or support to help manage or improve symptoms. These individuals were suffering from the myriad of clinical conditions and diseases resulting in loss of memory, executive function, and other features of cognitive impairment i.e. all components of our "thinking ability".

Some of these conditions can be reversible if diagnosed early e.g. anxiety, depression, endocrine disorders or may be progressive, including Parkinson's, Alzheimer's, vascular dementia or due to infection, trauma and many other causes. In addition, the neuro-developmental and autistic spectrum disorders presenting in children, will be more responsive to treatment, if recognized early. Advances in intensive therapies have been shown to change the child's future.

In 2011, as we started Re:Cognition Health, the team was very aware of the ongoing and very exciting advances in clinical research, especially for Alzheimer's disease, the only leading cause of death still on the rise. The introduction of new diagnostic tests to assist an early and accurate diagnosis, together with new generation medications designed to slow down further progression of disease if given early, provided the potential opportunity to change the future for those suffering from this disease. And maybe a chance for a cure, for the biggest emerging socio-economic healthcare crisis due to the increasing prevalence of the most common condition causing dementia, in older age.

Re:Cognition Health was founded on passion, a great idea and an opportunity in the market. These have been the key ingredients to the success.

The journey over the last six years has been nothing short of hard work. There have been multiple challenges and personal compromises in order to invest in the success of the business.

Hard work and positivity have been key drivers to the success of Re:Cognition Health and everyone within the organisation works together to continue to improve the probability of its success. I firmly believe that a company, and especially a new company, can be only as good as the talent and commitment of the people within the company. So, the most important challenge was and continues to be the search for the right people.

Goal Timelines

Goal setting has been an integral part of the business development. My vision is to have a global network of centres offering Re:Cognition's services. But growing a business on this scale takes time and a considerable financial investment. On a daily basis it's the smaller goals which we put in place to achieve, continually, which are required to keep the focus to achieve success. Benchmarks to monitor performance and progress are critical to keep on-track to realise the end goal. The Re:Cognition Health concept was an unproven entity and although we knew we had a great idea, there was always uncertainty as to how the concept would be received by the industry and the public.

The first goal was to secure funding to develop the idea, secure a location and get the company up and running. After a small investment round, we secured our first premises at Queen Anne Street, in the Harley Street Medical Area. We then began creating a network of industry-leading and internationally-recognised consultant clinicians to practice with us - a team of likeminded pioneers who shared our passion for medicine and the vision for our patients.

At the end of every single day, I ensure I have prioritised and completed at least three actions to move further towards the end goal. It's easy to get caught up in the day-to-day business operations, but I am always very conscious that every hour of every day matters. Sometimes actions can be very minor, but still very impactful on securing a successful outcome.

In October 2013, Re:Cognition Health started the first international trials for Alzheimer's disease; a culmination of focus, determination, relationship building and developing the right operational infrastructure.

Since the delivery of these contracts with the pharmaceutical companies, Re:Cognition Health achieved and maintained the top position, globally, for enrollment of individuals for several international studies. This achievement not only enhanced, significantly, the total UK enrollment performance, but also provided the chance for record numbers of UK patients (private and NHS) to have the potential opportunity to change their future by hopefully modifying the trajectory of their disease.

Whilst I stay focused on achieving goals to an agreed timeline, it's important that this remains flexible. The world is changing every day with advances in technology and consumerism, new discoveries, studies and reports. It's important to stay on top, well-informed, absorb information, read, adapt to the changing world and keep updating the goal timeline to reflect these changes.

Many of the Re:Cognition Health goals have been achieved earlier than forecast whereas other opportunities have not been as straightforward as originally envisioned. Measuring our output as carefully as possible has assisted us in making decisions to alter course and take advantage of relatively unforeseen opportunities. I believe firmly that "if you can't measure it, you can't improve it!"

In 2021, Re:Cognition Health will not resemble exactly the initial 10 year plan Tom and I forecast for the company in 2011, but it is not completely different and we are on target to exceed our initial objectives, several times over.

Determination

Determination has been fundamental to the success of Re:Cognition Health, approaching each day with mantras: **keep your eye on the prize** and **never give up**. There have and always will be, an abundance of hurdles and obstacles, especially in the field of medicine and clinical trials. It takes drive, ambition and determination to conquer these. For example, for the industry leaders with whom we work, there have been several failed clinical trials in Alzheimer's disease. This has been very disappointing for all involved, but especially for our patients and their families. Often many patients had perceived vast improvements in their symptoms and a failed trial comes as a surprise and with disappointment. The brain is possibly the most complex organ in the body, so there is a great deal which is not known and understood. Whilst it is very disappointing when hopes are dispelled with a failed trial, we must take solace in the fact that we learn something new with each study, getting us closer to understanding more about the disease, taking us closer to finding new treatments and ultimately helping to find a cure. Research and knowledge are power, but it is a long journey.

With Alzheimer's disease, we are currently at the point where cancer was several years ago and we must continue to trail blaze. As in all walks of life, a fail is rarely an endpoint. There are almost always positives and learning that can be drawn from each experience. I believe that how one deals with failure is possibly one of the key determinants in ultimately being successful. A person that never failed never tried. Determination to learn and to continue, is the key to success.

Confidence

Confidence and self-belief are instrumental to success, but believing one's own hype and seeking fame and attention is a distraction from the goal. Like in Greek mythology, hubris invariably leads to downfall. It's important to be honest with yourself, self-critical and analytical – always ask yourself how could you do better, even when you have done an outstanding job. I often have people comment on the lectures and presentations I give, however, I am always keen for feedback; has anything been missed, is the content relevant to the audience, should any topics be expanded? We pay careful attention to our patient and colleagues' feedback and continually strive to improve, paying attention to detail and to criticism.

Similarly, recognition for hard work, effort and excellence must be acknowledged at a personal level and we do compete for external competitive awards. Not only is it motivating for the person, team or business, but external acknowledgement can help further drive success.

Passion

Doing things for other people and for the greater good is extremely rewarding. Seeing the positive impact that effective treatment and care has on patients at Re:Cognition Health is extremely rewarding and is a driving force. We want to continue expanding the Re:Cognition Health business by opening new clinics in the UK and beyond so more people may benefit from the service, whether this be a child with autism, an adult with traumatic brain injury or a person with Alzheimer's disease. By truly loving the work and believing in it, work doesn't feel like work, it is a joy.

People and positions

It's important to evaluate people around you. What are they contributing? Are they the best person for the job? Are they in the best job to suit their skill set and temperament? Are they productive and happy? Having the right people in the right positions, with the right skill set and set of values, doing the right jobs has been imperative to the success and growth of Re:Cognition Health. There have been times when I have taken on too much and it's equally important to sometimes share the driving. I certainly don't have all of the answers, but we always find them when sharing with the team. I firmly believe that no one person has the monopoly on good ideas!

As well as setting business goals, it's also important to set personal KPI's for yourself and the team which should be reviewed on a regular basis. This will keep progress and productivity in check.

Eat for success

A healthy mind and body is essential to being successful, which means eating properly, exercising, having down time and leading a healthy lifestyle. When your mind and body are in good order, you can think more clearly - putting your business in good order to help achieve success. A healthy and well-rested mind is your best weapon, a mantra that we also employ for our patients. Research is providing increasing evidence of the benefits of good nutrition and a healthy lifestyle on current and future brain function.

Running a business can be very stressful so it's important to have down time to avoid burnout and take time to relax, but just don't relax or lose focus on the job!

Every day's a school day

The business world is changing very quickly with new systems and programmes to increase productivity. *If it ain't broke, don't fix it* is not the motto to have – standing still won't move you anywhere so be curious, ask questions, be inspired by other business models, attend conferences, network and never stop learning. It's also good to share information to help the industry improve. This can also have other positive implications such as increasing brand awareness, industry credibility and presenting new opportunities. Every month consultants from the Re:Cognition Health lecture and give presentations on a wide range of subjects to keep the clinic at the forefront and to help the industry learn and grow.

Dr Emer MacSweeney

About the author

Dr Emer MacSweeney is a leading London Neuroradiologist with experience in both the NHS and the independent sector. Currently, she is the CEO and Medical Director of Re:Cognition Health. Re:Cognition Health, is recognised as the UK's premier independent sector provider of cognitive services, both by its referrers and patients and has received multiple national and international awards. Re:Cognition Health's Centres are recognised, globally, as leaders in providing access for individuals to enrol on international clinical studies for new medications for Alzheimer's Disease.

Previously Dr MacSweeney was Director of Neuroradiology at Atkinson Morley's Hospital, St George's Healthcare Trust. She trained in neuroradiology at The Hospital of Neurology and Neurosurgery, Queen's Square, specialising in interventional vascular neuroradiology, and spent time on a scholarship at Harvard University. Dr MacSweeney has a special interest in neuroradiology of cognitive impairment disorders with considerable experience in imaging of neurovascular diseases and traumatic brain injury.

Printed in Poland
by Amazon Fulfillment
Poland Sp. z o.o., Wrocław